BENEDICT ON CAMPUS

EIGHT SPIRITUAL DISCIPLINES FOR COLLEGIATE MINISTRY

DAVID E. MACDONALD

Benedict on Campus: Eight Spiritual Disciplines for Collegiate Ministry

The General Board of Higher Education and Ministry leads and serves The United Methodist Church in the recruitment, preparation, nurture, education, and support of Christian leaders—lay and clergy—for the work of making disciples of Jesus Christ for the transformation of the world. Its vision is that a new generation of Christian leaders will commit boldly to Jesus Christ and be characterized by intellectual excellence, moral integrity, spiritual courage, and holiness of heart and life. The General Board of Higher Education and Ministry of The United Methodist Church serves as an advocate for the intellectual life of the church. The Board's mission embodies the Wesleyan tradition of commitment to the education of laypersons and ordained persons by providing access to higher education for all persons.

Wesley's Foundery Books is named for the abandoned foundery that early followers of John Wesley transformed, which became the cradle of London's Methodist movement.

Benedict on Campus: Eight Spiritual Disciplines for Collegiate Ministry

HIGHER EDUCATION & MINISTRY
General Board of Higher Education and Ministry
THE UNITED METHODIST CHURCH

For Kelly, who has supported my journey,
even when it didn't make sense.
And for the members of NACUC and UMCMA, who inspire me
to be a better chaplain and collegiate minister.

CONTENTS

PREFACE

YOU ARE ALREADY AN EXPERT (BUT YOU SHOULD READ THIS BOOK ANYWAY)

This book is for experts. Please don't stop reading, because if you are reading this, you are already an expert! Every person who is involved in leading, planning, or resourcing collegiate ministry is an expert in what works (and what doesn't work) in his or her particular context for ministry. As you read, you will find some ideas and concepts that will be new for you, and you may decide to try them out. Some will work; others will fail spectacularly. Congratulations! You've just learned something new about your context and become even more of an expert than you were before. You may find some practices that you have tried before, but they didn't work out with a specific group of students or at least didn't work as you intended. It can't hurt to try them again, because every cohort of students is different. What worked ten, five, or even two years ago may not work anymore, and what didn't work before might ignite a spiritual movement on your campus the likes of which you couldn't have imagined in your greatest dreams.

> Spiritual traditions of the church provide an anchor for emerging adults.

Every person who picks this book up has done so because he or she cares about the young people on our college and university campuses. You may be a chaplain, staff member in a spiritual life center, diversity officer, campus minister, para-church ministry organizer, or local church pastor or lay leader who has already started or is interested in starting a ministry of spiritual formation among college students. I write "among" and not "for" or "to" because you know that college students are naturally inclined toward active involvement in whatever organizations or ministries they happen to be involved. If you are a pastor, chaplain, or campus minister, you may find that the best way to implement this book is to put it in the hands of your student leaders, facilitate a group study of the book, and then let them loose to do what they will with what they have learned. I hope no one ever tells our supervisors how easy collegiate ministry really is!

If that last line got you laughing, then you really are an expert, because you know that it's not as easy as all that. In fact, collegiate ministry takes patience, goodwill, and the ability to mentor students through both successes and failures, and to rely often on sometimes-unreliable people whose schedules outside of your ministry setting often dominate their lives. You know that collegiate ministry is mostly about helping young people navigate the treacherous waters of emerging adulthood and supporting them as they make the inevitable mistakes that will lead to greater learning in the long run. As one of my student affairs colleagues once said, "You will be successful in working with students if you are able to watch different people make the same mistakes over and over again and still love them at the end of the day."[1] If you love your students, or if you are a student who loves your collegiate ministry, then you will know exactly what that means. So often, our ministry is one of bearing witness to the life changes, mistakes, and joys of emerging adults. We frequently feel as if we are not making much of a difference, but it only takes a moment or two of reflection to see how our ministries profoundly impact the lives of the students we love. It is my hope that this book will provide some pertinent resources for those ministries.

Throughout this book you will read stories from both the monastic tradition of the church, from which most of the disciplines highlighted here come, and from contemporary collegiate ministries, where these practices are being carried out today. After extensive interviews with colleagues who work as chaplains and campus ministers, I found myself with far too many stories for just one book. If what you read here inspires you, or if you wonder why I didn't include the spiritual disciplines that have given life to your collegiate ministry, I encourage you to write me—I'd love to get to know you and your ministry. Who knows? Perhaps another book will be in order down the road. For now, I had to limit myself to the eight most compelling examples of how classical spiritual disciplines are being used in collegiate ministry, framed

---

1   Many thanks to David Dellifield, director of the McIntosh Center at Ohio Northern University, who once gave this answer to a question from an interviewee for a student affairs position. I have used this often as a way to describe what we do in higher education student affairs and collegiate ministries.

by the stories of those who have practiced them in real life. I hope that you find these stories compelling and illuminating.

One of the key roles that a chaplain or campus minister can fulfill for students is that of a spiritual director. Far beyond simply providing programming, pastoral care, and moral support, the collegiate minister is one who can come alongside students, faculty, and staff and help them process through the complex feelings, thoughts, and relationships of collegiate life. The long-held spiritual traditions of the church can provide an anchor in the midst of the liminal experience of emerging adulthood. Engaging in the classical spiritual disciplines allows students the opportunity to become a part of a rich tapestry of practices that have been part of the life of the church for centuries. Bringing these practices to collegiate ministry is one way to connect students to the rich heritage of the church and can deepen and broaden their understanding of their own spiritual lives as well.

> Engaging in the classical spiritual disciplines allows students to become a part of the tapestry of Christian practices and can deepen their understanding of their own spiritual lives. looking for "something more."

The study of spiritual disciplines has been influenced by a number of scholars over the years, and many schemas have been proposed to categorize and describe the practices that the term "spiritual disciplines" encompasses. Richard Foster's *Celebration of Discipline*, Robin Maas and Gabriel O'Donnell's *Spiritual Traditions for the Contemporary*

Church, and Marjorie Thompson's *Soul Feast* are but some of the better-known examples. However, none of these has dealt specifically with how spiritual disciplines can be utilized within collegiate ministry—hence, the book you have in your hands right now.

Whatever you do with this book, make sure the students are behind it. Don't read it without your students. If the students are behind the idea, it will go. If not, you will struggle and feel frustrated. For this reason I have added a section at the end of each chapter with discussion questions for groups. Use these as a guide to help your student leaders discern how they might best utilize the tools contained herein within your collective collegiate ministry. May the spiritual disciplines contained within this book become for you a source of personal and communal spiritual growth, and may your ministry flourish as you and your student leaders increase in faith.

November 16, 2017
Feast of St. Margaret of Scotland

INTRODUCTION

BENEDICT ON CAMPUS

Let us therefore now at length rise up as the Scripture incites us when it says: "Now is the hour for us to arise from sleep." And with our eyes open to the divine light, let us with astonished ears listen to the admonition of God's voice daily crying out and saying: "Today if ye will hear His voice, harden not your hearts." And again: "He who has the hearing ear, let him hear what the Spirit announces to the churches." And what does the Spirit say? "Come, children, listen to me: I will teach you the fear of the Lord. Run while ye have the light of life, that the shades of death envelop you not."

—From the Rule of St. Benedict

Saint Benedict of Nursia was born in the late fifth century to a noble Italian family and entered the religious life early on at the behest of his father. As he progressed through the ranks of monasticism, Benedict became increasingly frustrated with the worldly sinfulness that he saw in some of his fellow monks and sought to reform monasticism. After a period of living as a hermit, Benedict drafted a set of rules for monastic communities[1]—rules he believed would bring readers "back to him from whom [they] had once drifted through the sloth of disobedience."[2] Benedict implemented his *Rule* in the thirteen monastic communities he led in Subiaco, and ultimately in his monastery in Monte Cassino. Benedict died in the mid-sixth century, and since that time his *Rule* has become the standard of practice for Western monasticism. Most monasteries, abbeys, and convents today either follow the *Rule* or some adaptation of it. Benedictine communities can be found all over the world, and the influence of the practices that Benedict implemented in his communities can be found in the Roman Catholic Liturgy of the Hours and in many private and corporate spiritual practices today.

But why should a United Methodist minister who is a chaplain on a United Methodist–related campus, writing for a United Methodist publisher, recommend the work of Saint Benedict for collegiate ministries? Do we not have any writings of our own Mr. Wesley that could form the basis of our spiritual practices? I would argue that the church in which John Wesley lived and moved, as part of the Western Christian tradition, was profoundly impacted by the practices introduced or emphasized by Saint Benedict. John Wesley would recognize the practices in this book as being essential to the life of the Church, though he may have placed less

---

1   "Life of Saint Benedict," official website of Montecassino Abbey, accessed March 12, 2018, http://www.abbaziamontecassino.org /abbey/index.php/en/legacy/saint-benedict-life-montecassino.
2   Timothy Fry, ed., *The Rule of St. Benedict in English* (Collegeville, MN: Liturgical Press, 1982), 15.

emphasis on some practices he might have deemed too "popish" for his Anglican tastes.

In his "General Rules of Our United Societies," Wesley wrote that those who wished to be a part of the work of the people called Methodist would do well to pay attention to three rules:

> First: to do no harm
> Second: to do good
> Third: to attend upon all the ordinances of God[3]

It is the third category, that of attending upon all the ordinances of God, that I will focus on the most for this book, although the directives to do no harm and to do good will also make appearances from time to time. Chapters 2–9 will look at eight spiritual disciplines from the Benedictine tradition, while providing examples of how those disciplines can be brought to bear on the practice of ministry on college campuses and among emerging adults. These disciplines are as follows:

- community prayer (chapter 2)
- Lectio Divina (chapter 3)
- contemplative prayer (chapter 4)
- service (chapter 5)
- spiritual direction (chapter 6)
- pilgrimage (chapter 7)

---

3 "The Nature, Design, and General Rules of Our United Societies," *The Book of Discipline of The United Methodist Church* 2012, ¶104 (Nashville: United Methodist Publishing House, 2012).

- intentional community (chapter 8)
- hospitality (chapter 9)

Students who come to collegiate ministry settings are looking for "something more"—to go beyond the basics of Christian faith, and to dig deep into the big questions of life. They are challenged in the classroom to look beyond the subjects they are studying—why not do the same with their faith? This book will address how spiritual disciplines can be brought to collegiate ministries in both "big picture" (theoretical) and practical ways, offering stories of collegiate ministries and tips on how to incorporate disciplines into ministries. It is intended to be used as a guidebook, and as with any good guidebook, there are helpful ways and not-so-helpful ways to use it. One unhelpful way to use this book would be to see it as a prescription for what ails your particular collegiate ministry, or as a road map to success. There are some practices in this book that will go over extremely well in a particular setting, while others will fall flat. As a collegiate minister you will be able to determine how the material in this book can best be adapted to the context in which you serve. Feel free to mix and match disciplines or use the material you find here as a launchpad for further study, leading you to discover other spiritual disciplines that may be much more effectively utilized in your specific setting. With that in mind, allow me to give you some tips on how to use this book:

> Students who come to collegiate ministry settings are looking for "something more."

1. Don't try to do everything at once—pick a spiritual discipline that appeals to you or to your students and start there.

2. You don't have to read this book in order—pick and choose the chapters you will read, or read them in a different order than I have proposed, based on your preferences and what piques your interest.

3. Remember the words of G. K. Chesterton: "If a thing is worth doing, it is worth doing badly."[4] If you try something in this book and it fails spectacularly, then you've learned something—move on and try something else, or learn from your spectacular failure and try it a different way next time.

4. Don't be limited by current budgets, space, or programming. Think beyond what you've always been able to accomplish. Look for funding from annual conferences, GBHEM grants, or from the institutions you serve. Start small if you have to, but start.

As you work your way through this book, you may discover you want to learn more. At the end of the book I have provided some resources to get you started on each of the practices, including online and app-based resources that help bring Benedictine practice into the twenty-first century. Feel free to use the resources you find here as a jumping-off point for your own explorations of spiritual disciplines, both personally and as a leader of collegiate ministries.

---

4 G. K. Chesterton, *What's Wrong with the World*, Pantianos Classics (1910; n.p.: CreateSpace), 121.

1 WHAT DO WE MEAN BY SPIRITUAL DISCIPLINES AND COLLEGIATE MINISTRY?

Spiritual Disciplines

Many books have been written over the years that define spiritual disciplines as they lay out various ways of categorizing them. These books are useful and continue to be a source of inspiration for me and for many others who study the practice of spiritual formation. As a result there are also many definitions for what constitutes a spiritual discipline. Feel free to explore those resources if you'd like to supplement the definition that I'm about to offer. For the purpose of this book I define spiritual disciplines as the actions we undertake and the habits we form over a lifetime that help us develop our spiritual lives. That's a pretty broad definition, and I've made it intentionally broad to prove a point. That is, there is no such thing as a "spiritual life" versus a "regular life."

For years, Western culture has steered people toward thinking about their lives as being divided into two mutually exclusive parts—the spiritual and the regular (or temporal/physical). This is a false dichotomy that encourages Christians in particular to see themselves as spirits trapped within earthly vessels. One popular (though often misunderstood) dictum sums up this thinking: "We are not human beings having a spiritual experience. We are spiritual beings having a human experience." This is a wonderful sentiment, but in reality, we are *both* spiritual *and* human. (This is perhaps the real meaning behind the dictum anyway.) Seen in this way, spiritual disciplines are not set-asides from daily life but part and parcel of daily life.

In the Benedictine tradition all of life is a spiritual discipline. Monks work under the banner of *ora et labora* (prayer and work), and the day is divided evenly between times of personal prayer, communal prayer, and the manual labor that keeps the monastery going. Being a monk doesn't mean retreating from the world to pray all day—far from it! In a Benedictine monastery there is very little difference between the atmosphere when the community is at work and when the community is at prayer. A sense of purposeful serenity envelops the visitor to a monastic community, as those who engage in the monastic life are bathed in the prayer of the community, which washes over into every activity.

> Spiritual disciplines are the actions we take and the habits we form over a lifetime that help us develop our spiritual lives.

Spiritual disciplines are called disciplines for a reason—they are hard to maintain and integrate into daily living. For a spiritual practice to go from being a special set-aside moment that is different from the rest of one's life to being an integral part of life, discipline is required. This may mean rearranging your daily schedule to accommodate your practices, or it may mean finding ways to integrate your practices into the routines you've already established in your life to make them part of (rather than separate from) your regular work.

According to the Benedictine mind-set, prayer and work are not distinct but part of each other. How we interact with each other in community, how we go about our work, how we interact with our bodies, and the spaces we inhabit are all involved in this conversation as well. Spiritual disciplines aid us in seeing the world as being in an ongoing relationship with God, and the regular practice of spiritual disciplines can help us order our lives in a way that will align us with God's will and priorities for the world. Prayer is work, and work is prayer, if we give both over to God as part of the ongoing conversation between the Creator and the creation.

To expand on this definition, let's examine some truths concerning spiritual disciplines:

- They are learned from a specific tradition. Spiritual disciplines did not spring out of nowhere. They have their roots in specific spiritual traditions and communities, and to fully appreciate the depth of the various disciplines and their usefulness for spiritual growth, we must first learn about the traditions from which they came.

- They are honed and practiced in a community of faith over time. There may be "spiritual superheroes" out there who believe they can practice spiritual disciplines by themselves, but most people find that the context of community is necessary to maintain the disciplines over a lifetime of practice. Even Thomas Merton, who desired more than anything to spend time in the hermitage at Gethsemani, still lived his life in the context of a monastic community. Time is the second crucial element here: No one becomes proficient at practicing a spiritual discipline overnight. As with learning to play an instrument or becoming proficient at any task, repeated practice of the spiritual disciplines is key.

- They may or may not have short-term measurable effects. Spiritual disciplines do not come with a lot of instant gratification. It may take many sessions, or even many years, before you can begin to see any demonstrable effects from your practice of a particular discipline.

- They become part of your life. Again, spiritual disciplines are not separate from ordinary life but part of it. They are not distractions, or even something for which time should be "set aside," but part of a daily routine. Perhaps the best sign that you are on track with practicing a spiritual discipline is that you sometimes find it boring. Boring isn't bad; it just means that you've integrated something into your life thoroughly—so thoroughly, in fact, that you can become bored with it! Boredom then becomes a sign not that your practice is ineffective but that it may be time for you to grow to a new level of depth in your practice.

Collegiate Ministry

The term I prefer to use for what we do when we work with emerging adults in higher education is *collegiate ministry*, because it encompasses all the various forms that such ministry takes. Some of the people I consider my colleagues in ministry are campus ministers, who work either in a local church or in an off-campus ministry, such as a Wesley Foundation or ecumenical campus ministry, which reaches out to students on secular state campuses. Others do their ministry in a sectarian environment, where they are called to be the campus pastors or priests to a specific faith community on a faith-based campus. Still others are chaplains at private colleges or universities who may come from a specific faith tradition but are called upon to work with students and faculty from a wide variety of faiths and world perspectives. Finally, there may be others who work for para-church organizations (like Cru or CCO) alongside student leaders on different kinds of campuses as they recruit and train members for their particular ministry.

Seen in this way, the term *collegiate ministry* is inclusive of those who work with people who are roughly eighteen to twenty-six years old and engaged in some way in furthering their education beyond high school. I like to think that we are all in this ministry together, and while we may have some distinct ways of doing our work that differ from context to context, we have more in common than not.

One of the goals of this book is to combat what I consider three misconceptions about the primary function of collegiate ministry. The first is that collegiate ministry is primarily a form of evangelism. This view of collegiate ministry places a high priority on the chaplain or campus minister being a conduit for helping students make a decision of faith—a conversion to Christ. The mission "to make disciples of Jesus Christ" is part of the overall mission of The United Methodist Church, but it is by no means the only function of collegiate ministry. To see collegiate ministry only as a means for evangelizing the current generation of college students is to only see part of the whole picture.

The second misconception is that collegiate ministry is primarily focused on social justice and radical hospitality. This is expressed in campus ministries that focus their efforts on helping students recognize the injustices that exist in the world and using the moral influence of the Christian faith to bring about change and right the wrongs of society. Again, this is only a part of what campus ministry can do. Focusing solely on this aspect can lead to a narrowly focused approach to collegiate ministry.

A third approach is that of collegiate ministry as "youth group, part two." In this model, collegiate ministry is a grown-up version of youth ministry in the same way that Dave & Buster's is a grown-up version of Chuck E. Cheese's. This kind of collegiate ministry is focused primarily on programming, fellowship, and reaching out to like-minded students who want a repeat during their college years of what they experienced during their high school years. This approach is fraught with problems, as Mark Oestreicher describes in his book *Youth Ministry 3.0.*[1] An effective collegiate ministry will have a mixture of all three of the aforementioned elements to varying degrees. I would also argue that for collegiate ministry to most effectively reach emerging adults, the practice of spiritual disciplines needs to be added to this list. Like a monastic community, collegiate ministries are poised for balancing evangelism, working for justice, fellowship, and the practice of spiritual disciplines, which makes for well-rounded individuals with a robust understanding of their faith.

Higher education has its roots in medieval monastic communities. In fact, many of the earliest colleges and universities in Europe were founded by monastic orders to educate and prepare their members and clergy for a life of service. The rhythms of monastic life (convocations, processions, feast days—even bells that mark out the hours) can still be found on university campuses today. Our academic regalia have their origins in monastic traditions, as do many of the terms we use for offices—dean, chancellor, and

Fun Fact: Saint Benedict was a twin. His sister, Saint Scholastica, is credited with implementing many of her brother's monastic reforms among monastic women.

---

1   Mark Oestreicher, *Youth Ministry 3.0: A Manifesto of Where We've Been, Where We Are, and Where We Need to Go* (Grand Rapids, MI: Zondervan, 2008). In this book, Oestreicher points out that a youth ministry that is built on a one-size-fits-all approach to programming is ineffective in reaching youth. He advocates for a relationship-building model of youth ministry, centered around developing authentic youth identity, autonomy, and affinity.

professor—and their liturgical and ecclesiastical purposes are echoed in how we still order campus life. The second goal of this book, then, is not just to introduce spiritual disciplines to collegiate ministry, but in a way to *reintroduce* the practices that are part of our spiritual and educational DNA.

Questions for Reflection

1. What spiritual disciplines, if any, do you currently incorporate into your collegiate ministry? Which ones do you find yourself connecting to the most on a personal level? Why do you think that is so?

2. What difference might it mean for your students to understand that they are both spiritual and physical individuals?

3. What is your response to the three misconceptions of collegiate ministry noted in this chapter? Do you agree or disagree that these are misconceptions about collegiate ministry? How might you define collegiate ministry as it is currently practiced in your setting? How might your definition change as a result of what you have read here?

4. If we accept that the collegiate setting has been greatly influenced by the practices of intentional communities, like the monastic communities founded by Saint Benedict, then what impact does that have on the way we see our collegiate ministries? What impact might that have on the way we approach campus life in general?

2 COMMUNAL PRAYER

The monks of the Abbey of Our Lady of Gethsemani in Bardstown, Kentucky, arise every day at 3 a.m. for the ancient Office of Vigils—the prayer of the night watch. It is the beginning of their day, which focuses on a cycle of prayer and work that lasts until they go to bed at 8 p.m. The sanctuary of their church is dark and cool—especially so during the winter. As each brother enters, he crosses himself with holy water from containers placed near the doors, and then he crosses the nave, pausing to bow before the altar, and finds his seat in the choir stalls that line the long, narrow nave. Those guests of the monks who wish to participate in their prayer time sit behind a low metal barrier that separates them from the monks. Each guest follows along with the prayer using a specially made booklet—one for each day of the week. This pattern repeats itself on a regular cycle of prayer throughout the day, through Lauds, Terce, Sext, None, Vespers, and Compline. At Compline, the abbot blesses all the brothers and guests with holy water, with prayers for a holy night of rest.

Introducing Communal Prayer

Many Christians will be familiar with the concept of praying with a group of other Christians. This is a common practice among all denominations and sects within the church. What some, including most Protestant Christians, will not be familiar with, is the type of communal prayer practiced in the Benedictine monastic tradition. Saint Benedict took the biblical injunction to "pray without ceasing" (1 Thessalonians 5:17) very seriously and believed that the daily life of his monks should be centered around prayer. Thus, Benedict identified seven times throughout the day when the monks should gather together for prayers, and he outlined the prayers and psalms that should be read during those times. Most monastic communities today follow the pattern of prayer set by Saint Benedict, although some communities have combined some hours of prayer and lessened the number of times the community gathers to five or in some cases even three times per day. These daily prayers are known as the "Liturgy of the Hours," or the Divine Office, and in communities that practice this most strictly (like the Trappists), the community will pray through all 150 psalms over the course of a week. Other biblical prayers, such as the Benedictus (Zacharias's prayer), the Magnificat (Mary's prayer), and the Nunc Dimittis (Simeon's prayer) are sprinkled throughout the Hours, as are regular intercessions for the needs of the community and the world. Most monastic communities follow some sort of breviary, which is a book containing all the Hours and their associated prayers, along with prayers and readings for special days, such as saints' feasts, Christmas, and Easter.

Putting Communal Prayer into Practice at the University of Indianapolis

At the University of Indianapolis (UIndy), Rev. Dr. Jeremiah Gibbs leads a small group of students, faculty, and staff in daily prayer, drawing on the tradition of monastic communities like the one at Gethsemani. Gibbs was inspired to start a practice of daily prayer on his campus after returning from the General Board of Higher Education and Ministry-sponsored *Novum* retreat, held at the Abbey of Gethsemani in 2016. As he thought about what he might do to bring a part of his experience at the abbey back to the campus, he wondered, "What would it look like if we took part of the Liturgy of the Hours from the monastic tradition and practiced it here?" Out of that came a daily midday prayer gathering, using a version of the ancient liturgy of Sext, the midday prayers in the monastery.

The UIndy liturgy is modernized, utilizing a contemporary version of the Gloria Patri, for instance, and includes a time for sharing prayer concerns just before the prayers of intercession. Gibbs has tasked one of his student staff members with compiling the liturgy for each day, and often leads the prayer himself, although others will sometimes fill in if needed. Attendance ranges anywhere from four to twelve, including students, faculty, and staff. The students on his staff get the word out about daily prayer through social media, and each day they post a list of prayer concerns on Twitter. Often, daily prayer includes one of the university's sports teams, which sparks a retweet from the account for the team being prayed for, widening the audience of those invited to prayer. In reflecting on his group's practice after a little over a year together, Gibbs noted that midday prayer has become very important in the lives of a small group of students involved with the chapel ministry, and that it has become an important part of his own spiritual practice as well. The midday liturgy has become a tradition at UIndy that has helped those who have participated grow in their faith and has reintroduced an ancient practice of the church to a modern audience.

> Communal prayer creates community between human beings and God.

Implementing Communal Prayer in Collegiate Ministry

Communal prayer is an experience of creating community between human beings and God, facilitated by the shared experience of praying the same words together or uniting the intentions of a group into one cohesive unit. By practicing this spiritual discipline together, the members of collegiate ministries are connecting themselves with a long tradition of gathering to pray with others. Communal prayers are most powerful and poignant when shared by a community experiencing grief, loss, or trauma, such as when a community member has died, but other occasions may call for communal prayer as well. For instance, communal prayer may be a way to unite people from across denominational lines to share with one another in Christian cooperation. Sometimes the obstacles of sharing in common worship, such as denominational differences, can be overcome when a group of students creates its own shared prayer liturgy or form.

Communal prayer has been helpful in our practice of ministry at Ohio Northern University in providing space for those students, faculty, and staff who do not connect well with the more contemporary style of our weekly worship gathering. As a result, this small but dedicated group meets weekly to pray together, utilizing a format that has been assembled from a variety of the rich liturgical resources available to the ecumenical church. This group has primarily served faculty and staff, but there are some students who, when they find out about this group, are relieved that there is a more liturgical option for them on campus and gladly take part each week. Below are two examples of some of the liturgies we have used for weekly prayer within our group. Feel free to adapt them or use them as they are.

The first liturgy is our regular weekly prayer format. I have included here the prayers, hymns, and readings for a particular saint's day—in this case, Aidan of Lindisfarne— but many of the elements of the service change from week to week, depending on the season or saint being celebrated. I use a variety of resources, including *The United Methodist Hymnal,* various breviaries, calendars of saints, and books of prayers, to populate each week's service. Hymns are sung a cappella, but you could certainly sing them accompanied if you had the talent available. The service also includes a time for silence, during which the participants spend some time reflecting on a question related to the theme of the day or the scripture readings. The service is meant to last about a half hour, but it could be lengthened or shortened depending on your needs.

Ohio Northern University, English Chapel, Order for Weekly Prayer

St. Aidan of Lindisfarne—31 August

Welcome and Greeting

Opening Response—

> Leader: O Lord, open our lips,
>
> **All: And we will declare your praise.**

Hymn or Song: **"Be Thou My Vision" #451**[1]

Prayer of the Day or Collect

> Leader: The Lord be with you.
>
> **People: And also with you.**
>
> Leader: Let us pray:
>
> **All: Almighty God,**
> **who called Aidan to proclaim the gospel**
> **and be the spiritual leader of the people of Northumbria,**
> **inspire in us the vision**
> **to preach the gospel in our time and place,**
> **through Jesus Christ our Lord,**
> **who lives and reigns with you and the Holy Spirit,**
> **one God, now and forever. Amen.**[2]

---

1 The hymn numbers refer to *The United Methodist Hymnal* (Nashville: United Methodist Publishing House, 1989).

2 This is a prayer that was written by me for this specific occasion, but we sometimes also include prayers from *Exciting Holiness: Collects*

Confession and Pardon

Leader: Let us confess our sins before God and one another.

All: Gracious God, have mercy on us. In your compassion forgive us our sins, known and unknown, those things done and left undone. Uphold us by your Spirit so that we may live and serve you in newness of life, to the honor and glory of your holy name; through Jesus Christ our Lord. Amen.

Leader: God is gracious and just, slow to anger and abounding in mercy. Therefore, we give thanks for God's saving grace!

All: Thanks be to God! Amen.

Psalter Responsive Reading: **Psalm 139 (UMH p. 854)**

Scripture Readings: **Isaiah 45:22–25 and 1 Corinthians 9:16–19**

Silent Reflection (To what lengths might you go if called by God to spread the gospel?)

Acclamation—(To end the period of silence)

All: Glory be to the Father, and to the Son, and to the Holy Spirit. As it was in the beginning, is now and ever shall be, world without end. Amen.

Communal Prayer[3]

Together let us pray for:

---

and Readings for the Festivals and Lesser Festivals of the Calendar of the Church of England (Norwich, UK: Canterbury Press, 1997).

3   This form is adapted from *The United Methodist Hymnal,* "Orders for Daily Praise and Prayer," pp. 876–79.

the people of this campus community…

Lord, in your mercy, **Hear our prayer.**

the concerns of this local community…

Lord, in your mercy, **Hear our prayer.**

those who suffer and those in trouble…

Lord, in your mercy, **Hear our prayer.**

our nation, the world, its peoples, and its leaders…

Lord, in your mercy, **Hear our prayer.**

the church universal—its leaders, its members, and its mission…

Lord, in your mercy, **Hear our prayer.**

the communion of saints…

Lord, in your mercy, **Hear our prayer.**

The Lord's Prayer

Hymn or Song: **"Be Still, My Soul" #534**

Final Blessing

Leader: May the grace of our Lord, Jesus Christ,
and the love of God,
and the fellowship of the Holy Spirit,
be among us, now and forevermore.

All: Amen.

We Depart in Peace

This next example is an order for prayer during final exams. I have used this with a group of students during finals week on campus as well as leaving copies of the liturgy in our prayer room during the same time. Groups are encouraged to pray this liturgy together as they prepare to take final exams, and the psalm and scripture readings could be changed from day to day or semester to semester, depending on the group's preferences. Finals are always a stressful time on any college or university campus, so gathering together for prayer can be an encouraging way to show your collegiate ministry's support of your students during what may be the most anxiety-prone part of their semester. One suggestion for utilizing this liturgy would be to lead it several different times during the week, in different locations around campus, so that students could attend at times that are convenient for them. Another idea would be to make this liturgy available online and encourage students to share in the prayer wherever they happen to be at certain times of the day or week, thus practicing the "communal" part of prayer.

An Order for Prayer during Final Exams

Invitation

O Lord, open our minds.

And our pens shall show forth knowledge and praise.

The Collect (In unison)

Almighty God, giver of all Knowledge and Wisdom,
we have come to a place where our knowledge must be tested
to prove that we have learned all we can.
Grant us the strength to endure long essay questions,
the clear thinking to tackle tough problems and formulae,

and the wisdom to rest between periods of intense
activity.
As you led the people of Israel through the desert,
show us a way
through this time of academic intensity,
that we may emerge on the other side, singing and
dancing
your praises, all the days of our lives.
Through Christ our Lord. Amen.

Psalm 34 (NRSV)

I will bless the Lord at all times;
his praise shall continually be in my mouth.
My soul makes its boast in the Lord;
let the humble hear and be glad.
O magnify the Lord with me,
and let us exalt his name together.
I sought the Lord, and he answered me,
and delivered me from all my fears.
Look to him, and be radiant;
so your faces shall never be ashamed.
This poor soul cried, and was heard by the Lord,
and was saved from every trouble.
The angel of the Lord encamps
around those who fear him, and delivers them.
O taste and see that the Lord is good;
happy are those who take refuge in him.
O fear the Lord, you his holy ones,
for those who fear him have no want.
The young lions suffer want and hunger,

but those who seek the Lord lack no good thing.

Come, O children, listen to me;

I will teach you the fear of the Lord.

Which of you desires life,

and covets many days to enjoy good?

Keep your tongue from evil,

and your lips from speaking deceit.

Depart from evil, and do good;

seek peace, and pursue it.

The eyes of the Lord are on the righteous,

and his ears are open to their cry.

The face of the Lord is against evildoers,

to cut off the remembrance of them from the earth.

When the righteous cry for help, the Lord hears,

and rescues them from all their troubles.

The Lord is near to the brokenhearted,

and saves the crushed in spirit.

Many are the afflictions of the righteous,

but the Lord rescues them from them all.

He keeps all their bones;

not one of them will be broken.

Evil brings death to the wicked,

and those who hate the righteous will be condemned.

The Lord redeems the life of his servants;

none of those who take refuge in him will be condemned.

The Song of Zechariah

"Blessed be the Lord God of Israel,

for he has looked favorably on his people and redeemed
them.

He has raised up a mighty Savior for us in the house of
his servant David,
as he spoke through the mouth of his holy prophets
from of old,
that we would be saved from our enemies and from
the hand of all who hate us. Thus he has shown the
mercy promised to our ancestors,
and has remembered his holy covenant,
the oath that he swore to our ancestor Abraham,
to grant us that we, being rescued from the hands of
our enemies,
might serve him without fear,
in holiness and righteousness before him all our days.
And you, child, will be called the prophet of the Most
High;
for you will go before the Lord to prepare his ways,
to give knowledge of salvation to his people by the
forgiveness of their sins.
By the tender mercy of our God, the dawn from on high
will break upon us,
to give light to those who sit in darkness and in the
shadow of death,
to guide our feet into the way of peace."
Glory be to the Father, and to the Son, and to the Holy
Spirit,
as it was in the beginning, is now and ever shall be,
world without end. Amen.

Gospel Reading: Luke 4:1-13 (Jesus is tested by Satan)

The Word of God for the people of God.

Thanks be to God.

Prayer

Together, let us pray:

for those who have exams in subjects they love, related to their major . . .

Lord, in your mercy,

Hear our prayer.

for those who have exams in subjects they loathe, unrelated to their interests . . .

Lord, in your mercy,

Hear our prayer.

for unfinished or poorly finished work . . .

Lord, in your mercy,

Hear our prayer.

for the grace to accept when we have completed our tasks . . .

Lord, in your mercy,

Hear our prayer.

for the strength to carry on and do what needs to be done . . .

Lord, in your mercy,

Hear our prayer.

for professors and instructors, who must grade our exams and papers . . .

Lord, in your mercy,

Hear our prayer.

for our families and friends, and stresses they may be going through . . .

Lord, in your mercy,

Hear our prayer.

> for those who are not privileged enough to have the
> opportunity to attend college or university . . .

Lord, in your mercy,

Hear our prayer.

> for the church and the world . . .

Lord, in your mercy,

Hear our prayer.

Lord's Prayer

Closing

Go now in peace, and as you learn more and more, may
you be blessed to know that you understand less and
less, and be comfortable knowing that God is in it all.
And may the grace of our Lord Jesus Christ, and the love
of God, and the fellowship of the Holy Spirit be with you
now and always. **Amen.**

Let us bless the Lord.

Thanks be to God.

Other Suggestions

Communal prayer doesn't have to take the form of a formal
liturgy. You could also gather students together for a time
of silent group prayer, with everyone focusing their individual prayers on a common theme. You might invite students
into a time of shared spontaneous prayers, allowing them to

express their thoughts out loud, or perhaps by writing their prayers out. For one chapel service at ONU, we invited students to take a piece of paper, write down their prayers, and then tape the piece of paper by their bathroom mirrors as a reminder to pray for their concerns each morning when they get ready for class. We have also encouraged students to pray together by writing their prayers on our campus "spirit rock," which had been painted to commemorate the National Day of Prayer. Gatherings for communal prayer on campus can be especially helpful during times of tragedy, such as following the death of a campus community member or a natural disaster. Following the death of a student on our campus, we gathered for prayer in the chapel and simply opened the floor to those who wanted to express their grief or pain and lifted the community up in prayer. Some shared lyrics from songs, and some shared bits of scripture that came to mind. It was a time for the entire community, from the president of the university to the students, to acknowledge our loss and seek a way forward together.

Whether you pray using a formal liturgy or you encourage a more free-flowing approach, communal prayer can have a powerful effect on a student community. In my first year at ONU, I conducted a series of one-on-one conversations with student leaders from across the Religious Life program. One theme that emerged from these conversations was the need for greater unity among the Christian organizations on campus. Later that year I called that group of leaders together for an evening of shared prayer around the theme of unity. Students were asked to pray in pairs, then to join with another pair and pray in groups of four, and then to come together as a whole to pray in unity. The mood in the room shifted noticeably, as students prayed first with people with whom they were very familiar, and then began branching out and praying with people they had never even spoken with before. The mood of divisiveness that existed in our community before that began to melt away as students shared their struggles, fears, and frustrations in prayer.

Out of that meeting, a number of new partnerships emerged. Two groups discovered that they were essentially doing the same things, and that they were trying to reach the same audience on campus, so they decided to merge into one new organization. Others realized that the different Christian groups on campus were more alike than they had previously thought and began to work on ways to hold events and social activities together. That one shared experience of prayer led our community to re-form a Religious Life Leadership Council on campus, which has since grown to represent all of the religious organizations, regardless of their faith traditions or theologies. Communal prayer has a way of bringing people together—quite literally.

Questions for Reflection

1. What forms of communal prayer, if any, exist within your collegiate ministry already? If you already have some communal prayer, how could you strengthen that practice? If you do not have any communal

prayer offerings, what steps do you need to take to begin something new?

2. After using one of the liturgical forms presented in this chapter, what are your reactions? At what moment(s) did you find yourself experiencing a closer connection to God and the people in your group? At what point did you feel uncomfortable or disconnected? Talk about that as a group—what might your experiences of this type of prayer be telling you?

3. What stories does your collegiate ministry have about the impact of communal prayer? How do you share those stories with others?

Fun Fact: The names for the Liturgy of the Hours and their meanings are:

Matins/Vigils (Early Morning)

Lauds (Praise)

Terce (The Third Hour—i.e., 9 a.m.)

Sext (The Sixth Hour—i.e., Noon)

None (The Ninth Hour—i.e., 3 p.m.)

Vespers (Evensong)

Compline (Complete—the end of the day)

---

3 LECTIO DIVINA

Before they could be mass-produced by the printing press, books (especially the Bible) were made by monks copying out the texts by hand. This was a slow and deliberative process, often involving the use of elaborate drawings, or "illuminations" within the text. These "illuminated manuscripts," such as the Lindisfarne Gospels or the Book of Kells, exist today as testimonies to the determination of our ancestors in the faith to keep the Word of God alive for future generations. As the monks copied out the texts of scripture, they naturally had plenty of time to reflect on what they were copying. This led to the development of a process of "holy reading," called by the Latin name Lectio Divina, which many people still practice today as a spiritual discipline. While we no longer need to copy out the texts of the scriptures by hand, we can still encounter the Word of God through deliberative reading and reflection.

Introducing Lectio Divina

In chapter 46 of the *Rule,* Saint Benedict wrote, "Idleness is the enemy of the soul"[1] and recommended both manual

---

1   Fry, *The Rule of St. Benedict in English,* 69 (see intro., n. 2).

labor and "prayerful reading" as a remedy to boredom and complacency and the attendant temptations to sin. The hours for reading that are set out in the *Rule* vary according to the seasons, probably owing to the difference in the amount of daylight in the winter and the summer. Benedict encouraged his monks to make reading an important part of their daily routine and often prescribed long periods of reading at certain times of the year, such as during Lent. The practice of extended periods of prayerful reading led to the development of Lectio Divina.

I first encountered Lectio Divina when I was in seminary, when my church history professor offered a lesson on the method of Lectio, and then shooed us all outside to reflect for a full hour on a scripture she assigned to each of us. I remember the experience well, because I was given one of the passages that has now become a standard for me when I introduce Lectio to others, "Be still, and know that I am God" (Psalm 46:10). I found myself slowly dropping a word from the end of the sentence with each repetition of the passage, so that it read something like this:

Be still, and know that I am God.
Be still, and know that I am.
Be still, and know.
Be still.
Be.

As I have worked with college students in my ministry on campus, I have introduced Lectio Divina as a way to reflect on Scripture without worrying about finding out what Scripture "means" or how it might apply to our current life situations. I incorporate Lectio into staff meetings, retreats, spiritual direction sessions, and any chance I can get in the course of ministry. During worship at our annual Religious Life staff retreat, we often utilize Lectio instead of having a sermon. In this way, all the members of our group have a chance to reflect on the scripture of the day and offer their thoughts, instead of hearing only one person's perspective. We have also used Lectio to help us reflect on sermons in chapel as part of our weekly reflecting time. One former staff member loved the practice of Lectio so much that when she asked me to read the scripture at her wedding, she requested that I do it in the style of our group Lectio practice.

There are four basic "movements" in the process of Lectio Divina, or as the ancient Carthusian writer Guigo II called them, four rungs on a ladder:

- *Lectio*, the process of reading through Scripture slowly and contemplatively
- *Meditatio*, in which the reader or listener is "transported" into the scripture, using his or her imagination to see the words of Scripture in a new light
- *Oratio*, a spoken prayer to God, based on the Meditatio stage, in which the prayer responds to God out of the call he or she is experiencing from this particular scripture
- *Contemplatio*, in which words are no longer needed, as the participant simply sits in silent contemplation of God's presence in the scripture and in his or her life

There are much longer and more precise explanations of Lectio than this one, but this basic flow from reading to meditation to prayer to contemplation is a format that can be adapted for a variety of situations and uses. The Bible is a natural resource for Lectio texts, but the method can also be used with other sacred writings, hymns, poetry, or even (gasp!) secular music.

Implementing Lectio Divina in Collegiate Ministry

For the purposes of introducing Lectio Divina to collegiate ministry, I recommend the following three practices:

First, Lectio could be introduced as a guided prayer experience. I have made a series of videos on various New Testament scriptures that lead watchers through a Lectio exercise. I uploaded the videos to YouTube and placed links on various social media pages related to our ministry. The script reads:

> **Blessings** to you, and welcome to this practice of Lectio Divina, or Divine Reading. In a moment, I will begin reading a passage of scripture. The passage will be read four times. After each reading, there will be a pause for reflection. If you feel you need more time to reflect, please feel free to pause the video and resume it when you are ready. Now, make yourself comfortable, and we'll begin.
>
> **Stage One: Lectio.** As the text is read aloud, listen and choose a word or phrase that stands out to you. When you find that word, repeat that word or

phrase out loud or silently to yourself. Think of its meaning. What does it mean to you? How is it striking you today? What might this word or phrase have to say to you in this moment?

Read: Matthew 21:28–32.

(Pause for reflection)

Stage Two: Meditatio (Meditation). During this second reading of the text, focus in on the word or phrase that you have chosen, noticing where it comes in the text. Meditate on what God might be saying through this particular word or phrase.

Read: Matthew 21:28–32.

(Pause for reflection)

Stage Three: Oratio (Prayer). During this phase, turn to God and speak, perhaps asking God a question about the word or phrase that you have chosen from this passage. You might think of asking God, "What are you trying to say to me?"

Read: Matthew 21:28–32.

(Pause for reflection)

Stage Four: Contemplatio (Contemplation). During this phase, you may find yourself falling into a state of contemplation. Experience the presence of the Holy Spirit, and resolve what you will do with what you have heard through this word of scripture. Say to God, "Now that I have heard you speaking, here is what I plan to do next."

Read: Matthew 21:28–32.

(Pause for reflection)

Glory be to the Father, and to the Son, and to the Holy Spirit. As it was in the beginning, is now and ever shall be, world without end. Amen.[2]

Second, we have used Lectio as part of group reflection exercises. Thanks to the work of Norvene Vest, a method for group Lectio Divina already exists, so I simply modified her method for use in our setting.[3] Here is an outline for how to practice Lectio in a group:

1. Choose a short passage of scripture to read, no more than two to three verses at the most. With more advanced groups, you may even be able to get away with only one verse.
2. Assign four readers, who will each read the passage one at a time, as instructed by the group facilitator.
3. Before the first reading, invite the group to listen carefully, particularly for a word or phrase that jumps out at them.
4. Have the first reader read the passage of scripture.
5. Ask the group, "What word or phrase sticks out to you in this passage?" Invite group members to speak

---

2   The entire series of these Lectio Divina videos can be found on You-Tube at: https://www.youtube.com/watch?v=bTkFbBdhzxO&list=PL9aGx6_wEb7feKWHq-G9v1olJ_yUZFvmT.
3   Norvene Vest, *Gathered in the Word* (Nashville: Upper Room Books, 1996), 27.

their word or phrase (without comment) into the center of the circle.

6. Invite the group to listen again to the scripture, focusing on the word or phrase they have each chosen, and asking, "What does this stir up within me?"

7. Ask the group, "How does this word make you feel?" Answer using phrases such as "I think," "I feel," or "I believe."

8. Invite the group to listen again, asking God, "What are you calling me to do with this word?"

9. Ask the group, "What is God calling you to do with this word? What change or action does the Lord ask of you?"

10. Invite the group to listen a final time, meditating on what their response might be to God.

11. Ask the group, "What will your response be to what you have heard here?"

12. Invite group members to pray for one another, each person focusing his or her prayers on the person to his or her right. As you go around the circle, group members are invited to pray, aloud or silently, each for the person to his or her right, and for the response that he or she lifted up to the group.

Group Lectio Divina can be a rich practice for a group of students, faculty, or staff to move out of the mode of reading Scripture for meaning or instructions. Unlike a Bible study or a discussion group, there is no intent here to come to a consensus as to what God might be saying in a particular passage of scripture. Instead, the focus is on supporting one another in prayer, which is itself focused on the words that have come from God to each individual and to the group as a whole.

Finally, the process of Lectio can be used to reflect on other media as well. For instance, you might try reflecting with students on a scene from a film. If using a film clip, all participants should have an understanding of what is going on in the clip. You might consider using a film that everyone in the group has already seen, or do the visual Lectio together after watching the film as a group. Here is an example of a visual Lectio:

> In the final scene of the film *Big Fish*, Will Bloom (played by Billy Crudup) tells his father, Edward (Albert Finney), a story in which he (Will) returns with Edward to the river where Edward was born. After a harrowing car drive through the city and out into the countryside, Will and Edward arrive at the river, to be greeted by all of the characters from the many tall tales Edward has told throughout his lifetime. Edward's old friends greet him and cheer as Will carries him to the water and places him gently into the current. Suddenly, Edward transforms into a giant fish and swims away. The scene cuts to Edward's funeral, where Will meets his father's old friends from back home. He is amazed to see that each of Edward's friends looks remarkably similar to one of the characters his father described in his fanciful stories, and he realizes that the stories his father told were more realistic than he had thought.

As a result, Will resolves to pass his father's stories on to his own son so that the family tradition of seeing the magic in everyday life can carry on.[4]

Have group members watch this scene, and then reflect on these questions:

1. What part of this film clip spoke most directly to you and why?
2. Place yourself in this story—do you identify with Will, who is carrying his father home for the last time? Edward, who is near the end of his life? The old friends who have gathered to say goodbye?
3. What lesson(s) about God can you discern from this clip?
4. Turn and speak with your neighbor about your thoughts and answers to these questions.
5. As a group: Where have we seen God in this clip?

Another way of approaching visual Lectio is to ponder a piece of art, such as a painting or a sculpture. This could easily be done by visiting a local museum, or if you are interested in reflecting on a famous piece of art, you could look for pictures of it on the internet. The process for reflecting on artwork is much the same as the ones described earlier. In addition to these, however, you might ponder the artistic medium chosen for the work, asking such questions as: Why might the artist have chosen this medium over others? In what ways does the chosen medium add to the message

---

4   *Big Fish,* directed by Tim Burton (USA: Columbia Pictures, 2003).

of the piece? For instance, if a sculpture is made of marble, the artist may have been choosing to say something about the formidability of the subject, or perhaps demonstrate the difficulty of producing something beautiful and delicate out of a hard stone. If a painter's brushstrokes are easily seen on the surface of a painting, perhaps you might reflect on how this technique makes the artist vulnerable to the world, since his or her methods are easily discerned and scrutinized. Ask yourself: "When have I felt vulnerable in my own work, and how did I handle that situation?" Through using different media, such as film and the fine arts, Lectio Divina can be used as a method for reflection on secular as well as religious works.

Lectio Divina can be a powerful way to connect students to Scripture and to the process of reflection in general. It is just as effective with students who are unfamiliar with Scripture as it is with those who have been Christians all their lives. Since the method relies on introspection, personal insight, and listening for the voice of God within, very little knowledge about the theology or mechanics of interpreting Scripture is needed, although it may lead students to express a desire to learn more about the Bible once they have encountered the power of God's Word. Many times, after a session of Lectio, a student will approach me and ask something like, "Where can I learn more about this passage?" or, "Are there other stories like this in the Bible?" Often they will be surprised at what they discover, perhaps because their past experiences with Scripture have been in the context of condemnation or judgmental faith communities.

Once, sitting on a bench by the shore of Lake Erie, I shared a session of Lectio on Psalm 46 with a young woman who was getting ready to go off to college. She had been through a pretty rough last year of high school and was seeking some help on where to go and what to do next with her life. As she repeated the words "Be still," her shoulders relaxed, and a smile spread across her face as she realized that, for perhaps the first time in her life, she was experiencing simply being present with God. There were no expectations laid on her to be the perfect daughter, sister, friend, or student leader. She wasn't the president of any club or the captain of any team, but a child feeling the loving embrace of her Parent. Lectio became for her a way of laying aside her burdens and taking on the yoke of Christ, which came as sweet relief after a trying adolescence. I have had the opportunity to witness this transforming effect many times over, as I have led young people in the practice of Lectio over the past several years, and every time it feels just as amazing as the first.

Fun Fact: Lectio Divina can be practiced alone or in groups and can use scripture, artwork, music, film, or any other kind of media. Your practice of Lectio is only limited by your imagination and your level of willingness to let go and contemplate God in your everyday life.

Questions for Reflection

1. What settings in your collegiate ministry would be most conducive to the practice of Lectio Divina?

What students can you identify who would be receptive to Lectio?

2. What barriers to the practice of Lectio Divina can you identify: within your campus setting, your specific ministry group, or the students with whom you work? How might you best work to overcome those barriers?

3. After practicing Lectio (individually or as a group), how would you describe your experience in one or two words? Why did you choose those words? What insights did you gain from the experience that you would like to share with others in your ministry group?

4 CONTEMPLATIVE PRAYER

The spirit of *Contemplatio* pervades Benedictine monastic communities, especially during times when the monks are silent. Each night, after the final prayers of Compline are sung and the abbot blesses the community, Benedictines practice what is known as the "Great Silence," a time when complete silence should be kept until the Vigils prayers in the morning. Following Vigils there is normally a shorter period of relative silence while the monks do their spiritual reading or Lectio Divina. In some monasteries silence is kept at all times, except when praying, attending to business, or looking after the needs of guests. These periods of silence allow for a kind of prayer that engages God through listening to the "still small voice" within and around a monk's life (see 1 Kings 19:11-13). Contemplative prayer is rooted in the idea that we can only truly achieve communion with God when we silence ourselves enough to hear God speaking to us. Much like the practice of silent worship in the Quaker tradition, there is an emphasis on the movement of the Holy Spirit in contemplative practice.

Introducing Contemplative Prayer

In the latter part of the fourteenth century, an anonymous monk or priest in England wrote a book called *The Cloud of*

Unknowing to provide advice for a young person wishing to find God. The author's main argument is that God's glory cannot be experienced through activity and study of the world but through complete surrender to God and contemplation. The author described the human inability to fully grasp God as "the cloud of unknowing," and wrote, "This darkness and cloud is always between you and your God, no matter what you may do, and it prevents you from seeing him by the light of understanding in your reason"[1]

Contemplative prayer is a natural companion to Lectio Divina, as the final step in the process, and the real, ongoing work of the practitioner of Lectio is to reach a point of contemplation where the mysteries of God's nature can be explored, unencumbered by thoughts or distractions. Thomas Merton, who practiced contemplative prayer as a member of the Trappist order, wrote that contemplative prayer is a companion to the active life of a Christian and that both activity and contemplation are necessary to live a balanced life. However, Merton added, "prayer, in order to penetrate more deeply into the mystery of God, must 'rest from the exterior action and cleave only to the desire of the Maker.'"[2]

In January 2016, a group of campus ministers and chaplains gathered at the Abbey of Gethsemani for the first *Novum* retreat sponsored by the General Board of Higher Education

---

1 James Walsh, SJ, ed., *The Cloud of Unknowing* (Ramsey, NJ: Paulist Press, 1981), 121.
2 Thomas Merton, *Contemplative Prayer* (New York: Doubleday, 1969; 1996), 52.

and Ministry office of Collegiate Ministry. The retreat was meant as a time for silence, reflection, and refreshment for those who work diligently to help college students in their spiritual growth. Most of each day was spent in silence, as is the tradition at Gethsemani, which is a Trappist monastery, but there were a few brief times during the week when the group got together for reflection and conversation. One of those times was a hike through the wooded hills surrounding the abbey.

We set out from the abbey on a cool but bright day and hiked up into the woods toward a very special destination—the hermitage that once housed Thomas Merton. It was a special honor to be able to visit the hermitage, since it is usually reserved for use by the monks as a private retreat—yes, even Trappists need to get away from it all from time to time! Our guide for the day was Brother Paul, who was a student of Merton's. As we approached the hermitage I was stunned at how different it was from what I had imagined. Even though I had seen pictures, I had imagined it would be much more rustic. There is no running water, and the only source of heat is a woodstove. Sturdily constructed out of cinder block, the building presents a beautiful view of the hill country below.

We were shown around the hermitage—it didn't take long, since there is only a front sitting room, a kitchen, a small bedroom, and a prayer space—and then went out to the porch to listen to Brother Paul tell stories about his mentor, Merton. At one point in the conversation Brother Paul said, "And here is the reason Merton chose this spot for the hermitage. First, it has the best views of the Kentucky hills for miles around. And second . . ." and then he trailed off into silence. We sat there together in that silence, not awkwardly, but in a companionable kind of silence like that shared between old friends. The silence led us into a peaceful sense of contemplation—a perfect tribute to the man who is considered by many to be their father in the practice of contemplative prayer.

As with the other practices included in this book, contemplative prayer has its roots in the monastic tradition. The monks who spent their days in prayer and the labor of preserving the sacred texts handed down to them by their ancestors in the faith often found themselves drawn into contemplative silence. Contemplative prayer has a particular appeal to those who consider themselves "spiritual but not religious," because its practice does not necessarily require one to adhere to a particular theological position. I have used contemplative prayer as a way to help students put aside their hang-ups about organized religion and focus instead on the presence of God.

> Contemplative prayer can be a way to help students put aside their hang-ups about organized religion and focus on the presence of God.

Contemplative prayer can be practiced either in a group or on your own; but either way it is best practiced under the direction of an experienced teacher or guide. Life and all of its distractions can cause us to quickly leave the contemplative mood and begin thinking about all sorts of issues: grocery lists, homework assignments, upcoming exams, and that fight you had with your significant other all have a gravitational pull of their own that can suck you out of contemplation very quickly. Having others with whom you can practice or a teacher who can guide you until you become proficient in this practice can be very helpful in avoiding distractions, although there is no foolproof way to do this, and distractions are an inevitable part of contemplative prayer. I find that the distractions I encounter when practicing contemplation can become a good source for the intentions that go along with my practice. If I find myself thinking of a person or an issue while engaged in contemplative prayer, I simply try to acknowledge the existence of what I'm thinking about and make my continued contemplation a way to help me focus positive energy and prayer toward that situation.

Implementing Contemplative Prayer in Collegiate Ministry

Contemplative prayer requires a good amount of silence, which can be a precious commodity on a college or university campus. I have found it useful to introduce contemplative prayer not during silent retreats in faraway settings but in the midst of the hustle-bustle of campus life. That way, students can get used to finding the inner quiet they need for contemplation, rather than relying on the conditions being just right. Spaces for meditation and contemplative prayer on campus can be helpful, though, in encouraging students to take some time out of their busy lives to experience some actual silence.

There are a variety of ways in which contemplative spaces can be set up on a campus or in a setting where students are engaged in campus ministry. At ONU, we have two dedicated prayer spaces that are open twenty-four hours a day during the academic year. One space reflects our Christian heritage specifically, while the other space is set up for use by people of all faiths. In the Christian prayer room we encourage silence through the use of low lighting, provided by a lamp and two stained glass windows that are artificially lit from behind. There are numerous bookcases with hymnals, prayer books, Bibles, devotionals, and commentaries available for anyone who needs them. In the center of the room is a circular prayer rail for those who wish to kneel while praying, and the outside edges of the room are ringed by padded benches. Our multifaith space is bright and airy, utilizing natural light from two skylights. The soaring wood ceiling gives a natural look to the room that draws one's thoughts and prayers upwards. To the left of the door as you enter the room, there is a shelf where users are asked to deposit their shoes—this is a strictly socks-and-bare-feet-only zone. A restroom is located nearby for those who wish to wash before praying, and a bookcase includes sacred texts from a variety of religious traditions. Prayer rugs and cushions are provided, as well as optional dividers, should a praying community have the requirement to separate the sexes during prayer.

Both of the prayer spaces described above are made available either to individuals who wish to drop by and pray or meditate or to groups who wish to book them in advance for special use. Our prayer room has been used by the Newman Club for praying the rosary and for our weekly liturgical prayer group. The multi-faith room has hosted Muslim prayer times, Jewish celebrations of Hanukkah, and even a pagan solstice prayer ritual. For those who are engaged in Christian-specific campus ministries, the idea of a multi-faith prayer space might seem unusual, but for those of us who are chaplains on campuses where multiple faith traditions are represented, having such spaces is a way of providing hospitality to our student bodies and lives out the golden rule in a unique way. Just as we would wish to have a space available for us to use for prayer, it is important for us to provide a space that can be welcoming for people of other faiths. This helps build trust and interfaith understanding on college campuses.

When providing spaces for prayer and contemplation, it is important to consider issues of safety for your students and community members. While our spaces are available twenty-four hours a day, they are frequently monitored by campus security, and a camera placed near the door records who is coming and going. Students are encouraged to be aware of their surroundings and to use the buddy system, if possible, when they enter the prayer spaces late at night. Our building is also designed so that the main sanctuary and the classrooms and office spaces in the building are locked off from the prayer spaces at night. This may not be possible in all situations, but it may be a factor to consider if you are adding a prayer space to your collegiate ministry. The key to offering contemplative prayer space is to have a space that is welcoming, hospitable, and safe. Some of our students have discovered that the prayer rooms on campus are safe spaces to reflect and study during finals week, and our custodian even found one student asleep in the multi-faith room when she came in one morning to open the building.

Contemplation and meditation are excellent ways to augment the current program offerings of your collegiate ministry as well. There is no need to create a new program just for contemplative practice when you can add this aspect to an existing program in a meaningful way.

In our ministry we often hold what we call "De-stress/ Refresh" events, which are generally held round the time of midterms or finals. These events are opportunities for students to unwind, have some fun, enjoy some home cooking or tasty treats, and integrate their spiritual life into their academic life. Our De-stress events are usually come-and-go in nature, with a starting and ending time listed in promotional materials, but no expectations for when students must arrive and leave. Some examples of contemplative practices we have incorporated into De-stress/Refresh include the following:

- a canvas labyrinth set up in a quiet classroom or in the library lobby
- a "quiet room," where students are encouraged to kick off their shoes, sit or lie down on the floor, and listen to some meditative music or ambient sounds
- a prayer station, which might include the practice of Lectio Divina, designed to draw students into a contemplative mind-set

The possibilities are limited only by the imagination of your ministry team.

A couple of lessons we have learned from incorporating contemplation into our events are worthy of noting here:

- It is sometimes difficult to get students to leave activities such as big-screen *Mario Kart* or Zumba to participate in quiet meditation. Think about the mix of activities you are offering and recognize that not everyone will want to participate in every offering.

- Having your contemplative zone set up with soft lighting, draped fabrics, or some kind of inviting atmosphere can help get students into the right frame of mind for contemplative prayer.

- It helps to have students who love sharing with others about contemplative practice to invite others to join them in the contemplative activity being offered.

- Recognize that contemplative prayer comes very easily to some people, such as introverts, but that others may struggle with silence or sitting still for long periods. We have offered prayer beads as a way for those who need a "fidget" to help them stay focused. Rather than seeing such items as distractions, they can become useful tools for contemplative prayer. Another helpful tool is the proliferation of "grown-up coloring books," which offer complex designs as an aid to meditation. Many coloring pages can be downloaded from the internet or purchased rather inexpensively from bookstores or gift shops. I keep a stash of coloring books and colored pencils, crayons, and markers, as well as a collection of other art supplies, on a bookshelf in my office. Students know that they can come by and borrow the materials anytime, as long as they take care of them and make sure they return them for use by other students. It's not unusual for one of my student leaders to stop by my office, walk in, and say, "I'm just here to borrow some Play-Doh."

Some students may enjoy your forays into contemplative prayer so much that they want to start a meditation gathering or contemplative prayer group. Contemplative Outreach is an organization that offers excellent resources on forming centering prayer groups. The works of Thomas Merton, Thomas Kelly, Richard Baxter, and Ignatius of Loyola as well as the previously mentioned *Cloud of Unknowing* are all excellent resources for going deeper into contemplative practice.

Emergency Mode Ministry

Those of us who are involved in collegiate ministry often find ourselves operating in "emergency mode" on a regular basis—dealing with the many personal issues our students bring to our offices, arranging meetings among people with very busy schedules, struggling against decaying buildings and infrastructure, or any of the other dramatic emerging issues that come with working alongside young people, who are still in the process of developing into their adult selves. It can be easy to descend into a kind of triage approach to ministry, in which we constantly struggle to determine which priorities are the most important and how we can stretch our ever-thinning resources to address them. While we teach stress management and reliance on God's grace to our students, we are often the last people to hear our own teaching and the most reluctant to apply those teachings to our own lives.

For these reasons, collegiate ministers of all types must ensure that they engage in the practices described in this book as part of their personal spiritual growth. Despite the warnings from Ezekiel 34 about shepherds feeding themselves at the expense of the sheep, it is still important that shepherds find some way to be fed. Otherwise, as my seminary advisor once told me, "the shepherd will become so weak that the shepherd either devours the sheep, or the sheep will devour the shepherd." Regular retreats and time away from your ministry are a "must-do" on your list as a collegiate minister. If you neglect your own spiritual growth in favor of the growth of others, then you will be no good, either to yourself or to others, and you will resent your work rather than relish it.

I believe that a good way for collegiate ministers to see themselves is as "professional contemplative practitioners." This means that we both engage in contemplative practices and teach them to others. Prayer and meditation are part of our work and should be the bookends for each day of our ministry. Students will be encouraged in their own devotional and contemplative practices if they see their leaders engaging in the same practices regularly, and particularly if their leaders are willing to share their struggles with maintaining their practices. Such vulnerability allows us to be seen as human beings, and our students will have a much easier time relating to us than to the super-together images that we sometimes try to portray.

Spiritual Direction Ministry

Because my training is in spiritual formation and spiritual direction, I see my ministry as being one primarily of spiritual direction. This way of looking at ministry can have a profound effect on the approach you take to others. I have found that even when I have been engaging in evangelism— reaching others with the gospel with the purpose of making disciples for Jesus Christ—it is most helpful for me when I see this as an act of spiritual direction. After all, I am not making disciples, but it is the Holy Spirit who works through me. The Holy Spirit is the true spiritual director, and we who are in ministry are conduits of God's work in the world. Collegiate ministry offers us the opportunity to live out that call to ministry in an environment where many people are still developing their sense of identity and place in the world. Contemplative practice gives us a way to come alongside them and encourage their development in a way that fosters greater faith in God.

The most profound effect I have personally witnessed from contemplative prayer has been within my own family. After a particularly difficult appointment to a church that was not a good match (for either me or the congregation), I was quite relieved when my district superintendent called me one day in January to tell me that the bishop intended to move me to a new church by the end of March. My wife and I were relieved to be free of the burden of struggling in a place where neither we nor the congregation could flourish, but we didn't anticipate the effect that such a sudden, midyear move might have on our young daughter. After the move, while we were settling in to our new parsonage and congregation, we noticed that our daughter was struggling with anger—lashing out at people without provocation. After some counseling, we realized that while my wife and I were ecstatic for our move, our daughter had only fond memories of the place we had left, in part because we had shielded her from the worst of what was going on. As part of her therapy, we were encouraged to help her practice meditation. After a few sessions of meditating together early in the morning before school, we found that she had a different outlook about school, family, and her peers. Over time, she has developed her own practice of meditation and enjoys a deeply rich interior life, the likes of which I may never know, but for which I am grateful every day. I have seen similar effects with students in my practice of ministry at ONU, and I am always astounded at the ways God reaches into the lives of those who seek a deeper relationship with the Divine Presence.

A Cumulative Process

Contemplative prayer does not come with immediately measurable results. It often takes time and lots of practice for contemplation to truly have an effect on one's life. We must make this point when introducing students to contemplative prayer, because we live in a world that expects instant results. Explain that contemplative prayer is a cumulative process—each session builds on the last, and each time we practice contemplation we are able to go deeper into the presence of God. Only after a long time of practicing contemplation can one begin to discern its effects, and these are sometimes subtle at best. Rather than discouraging the use of this practice, understanding that the process of growth is lengthy and may require many repeat attempts can be helpful. If one goes into the practice with the idea that it may take a great deal of time before results are evident, then the lack of outward and dramatic changes in one's life are not disappointments. Instead, the patience required to "wait for the LORD" is the greatest benefit derived from contemplation (Psalm 27:14 NRSV). In a world where we are constantly bombarded with quick-fix ideas, the idea of a contemplative life that measures growth in years rather than minutes or even days can actually be refreshing.

Fun Fact: Thomas Merton was briefly a college English professor at St. Bonaventure University before he entered the Trappist order of monks. Visitors to St. Bonaventure's rare books collection can view some of Merton's early journals.

Practicing Contemplative Prayer

Contemplative prayer can be practiced individually, with a spiritual director, or as a group. It is advisable to begin this practice under the direction of an experienced practitioner or in a group setting to avoid unnecessary feelings of inadequacy at first. It is normal to feel as if you're not doing things right when you first start out. Here is some advice from the ancient authority on the practice of contemplative prayer, *The Cloud of Unknowing:* "Do all that lies within you to forget all the creatures that God ever made, and their works, so that neither your thought nor your desire be directed or extended to any of them, neither in general nor in particular. Let them alone and pay no attention to them. This is the work of the soul that pleases God most."[3]

Questions for Reflection

1. What places in your life would make good entry points into contemplative prayer?
2. How do you deal with distractions during your contemplative practice?
3. In what ways might you use contemplative prayer in your ministry?
4. What immediate effects do you notice after practicing contemplative prayer? What longer-term effects have you noticed, or if this is your first time, what long-term effects can you imagine might come from this practice?

---

3   Walsh, *The Cloud of Unknowing,* 120.

5 SERVICE

The motto of the Benedictine orders is "Ora et Labora," which means "Prayer and Work," the two pillars upon which the Benedictine charism is founded. The apostle James wrote in the New Testament that "faith without works is dead" (James 2:20, 26), and Christians have known instinctively for centuries that a proper response to our salvation and new life in Christ is to serve others. Saint Francis of Assisi took the call to service one step further by radically identifying himself and the members of his religious community of friars with the poor, living lives of total poverty and giving all materials goods away to others. John Wesley urged his followers, "Earn all you can, and save all you can, so that you can give all you can," and the early Methodists founded orphanages, schools, and hospitals as ways to reach out in service and compassion to others in Christ's name.

Introducing Service

Service is a natural element of collegiate ministry. There are many ways to channel the energy and enthusiasm of young people into the practice of serving others. From a Benedictine monastic perspective, service is at the core of what makes the monastery work. This commitment to serving others begins with the abbot, who is charged with being the spiritual father of the other monks. The abbot should conduct himself in such a way that his actions show how a monk should live: he should refrain from that which he expects his monks to refrain, and participate in that which he would encourage among the brothers.[1] Similar job descriptions can be found in the *Rule* for deans of the monastery (chapter 21), the cellarer (chapter 31), readers (chapter 38), artisans (chapter 57), and the porter (chapter 66). Regarding kitchen servers (chapter 35), Benedict wrote, "The brothers should serve one another ... for such service increases reward and fosters love."[2] Those who work in the kitchen are to receive an extra portion of food and drink before mealtimes so that "they may serve their brothers without grumbling or hardship." Each Sunday morning, at Lauds, the abbot and the community bless those called to undertake the drudgery of kitchen work, to demonstrate how even the most menial of tasks can be seen as holy before God.[3] Service to others in the monastery may come easily, because the results of one's service can be seen immediately and up close. Service performed for guests, who often come and go and do not stay for very long, can be more difficult, as guests may sometimes be less grateful after a long and arduous journey, and

---

1   Fry, *The Rule of St. Benedict in English,* chap. 2, "The Qualities of the Abbot," 21–25 (see intro., n. 2).
2   Fry, 57.
3   Fry, 58.

the effects of one's service may not be readily discerned. Thus, monks come to learn that the service they render to others is not meant for their own enjoyment or goodwill, but so that all the glory may be given to God. I will say more about welcoming guests in chapter 9.

Implementing Service in Collegiate Ministry

Spring break is normally a time when college students let loose and de-stress from all the worries and deadlines that loom large in their lives during the semester. For those colleges in the northern part of the United States, especially, spring break can be a time when students can break free from the monotony of the ice and snow on campus and head for warmer climes for a little sun and fun.

One group of students with whom I have had the pleasure of serving in ministry over the past several years is our campus chapter of Habitat for Humanity. These students work hard throughout the year to raise thousands of dollars in order to travel south over spring break, not for the bars or the beaches, but for neighborhoods in desperate need of adequate and affordable housing. I have accompanied several groups of students to places such as Jackson, Mississippi; Birmingham, Alabama; Davidson, North Carolina; and Dade City, Florida. Each time I go on a Habitat trip with our students, I am amazed at the ways God works through them, even when they themselves are not aware of it. Prevenient grace flows freely in times of service, when we are able to be the hands and feet and presence of Christ even to those who do not share our faith.

Each evening during our Habitat trips, the group always sits down for a time of devotions, called a "Habi-Chat," and sharing around the circle, which is called "Roses and Thorns." Roses are the bright moments of the day, or when God's presence was felt most. Thorns are the less pleasant aspects of the day's work, such as a hammered thumb or a window frame that has to be taken apart and rebuilt because it doesn't meet the specs provided by the jobsite coordinator. Often this time of reflection leads students to more deeply understand the purpose of their service. Beyond just earning volunteer service hours for a class or major requirement, students come to realize that their service makes a difference in the lives of those around them, and within them as well.

Service may seem like a bit of a no-brainer for a book on collegiate ministry. After all, alternative spring break trips and mission trips abroad have been a staple of college-age and youth ministries for decades. That may be true, but many of us do not often think of service or mission opportunities as spiritual disciplines. The spiritual factor of service can be especially difficult to explore in settings where students might come from a variety of spiritual or religious traditions. Our Habitat for Humanity trips often attract non-Christian and even nontheist students, and many campuses host campus-wide days of service, which may include participants from a diverse cross-section of the campus community. This might be a good opportunity to have students share from their various traditions about what service means to them. I once witnessed a student from a non-Christian tradition who became curious about Christianity and wanted to learn more about the Bible because he saw how the Christian students on a work trip acted toward one another and toward the people they met on the trip. Interfaith work projects, such as those encouraged by groups like Interfaith Youth Core (IFYC), can be great opportunities for students to grow in their faith while also learning about the faith of others. Interfaith cooperation can have the effect of broadening students' thinking about their own faith traditions, causing them to explore their faith more deeply.

> Service provides ways for students to live out their faith in a concrete way. It gives them opportunities to reflect on their place in the world and what it means to be useful to others.

The Effects of Reflective Service

Service that is undertaken deliberately and with a reflective tone can become a meaningful spiritual practice for students and collegiate ministers alike. Not only does service offer the opportunity for students to live out their faith in a concrete way, it also offers opportunities for them to reflect on their place in the world and what it means to be useful to others. Service can also be a humbling experience, as students are made aware of the privileged position they hold by having the opportunity to receive an advanced education and the responsibility they have to serve others who are less privileged. Service should not, however, become an opportunity for voyeurism. Nor should service be a way for students to feel better about themselves because they have helped "those people" who are in need.

Service does provide the opportunity for meaningful engagement with others, relationship building, and partnership among equals. For instance, one of our Habitat groups has been going to Jackson, Mississippi, every spring break for more than twenty years, which has led to our university developing a deep and abiding relationship with the people of that city, the local Habitat affiliate, and the homeowners with whom the students have worked side by side in building new homes.

Perhaps already a part of your collegiate ministry, here are a few suggestions for making service a spiritual practice for your community:

- Appoint both a logistics leader and a reflection leader for each service group. The logistics leader's job is to make arrangements for transportation, lodging, and food, and to act as a liaison to the work site coordinator or local agency in charge of the service project. The reflection leader focuses on the group's morale during the project (including encouraging everyone to stay hydrated and fed) and leads discussions in both formal and informal ways throughout the project to help participants look more deeply at what they are doing as a spiritual practice and not just a "good deed." In my context, a student and a faculty or staff member respectively have traditionally taken these roles, but the roles could be reversed depending on the giftedness of the leaders involved.

- Make reflective activities engaging. If students look forward to reflection time, they are more likely to participate enthusiastically. "Roses and Thorns" has become a cherished tradition among our students, and other service groups on campus have adopted this practice as well. Utilize your team's creativity to come up with fun or appealing ways to facilitate reflection. Daily journaling with writing prompts or questions may help some students reflect on very personal encounters they have experienced during a service project, which they might otherwise not share with a large group. If the group is quite large, sharing might take the form of smaller groups reflecting at the end of the day with each other, and then presenting their combined reflections in the form of a skit or song. One form of reflection that is sometimes used when a group is intimately working and living together throughout a weeklong mission trip involves "warm fuzzy" bags. At the beginning of the week each participant decorates his or her own paper bag (for example, a lunch bag), or even a large envelope, and then places it in a prominent location in the living area alongside the other participants' bags. Participants are encouraged to write encouraging notes to one another throughout the week and place them in each other's "warm fuzzy" bags. The bags can be checked daily for any new "mail" or can be picked up all at once at the end of the week. In the latter case, it is helpful to give students their bags when they get home, to help them carry the experience of the mission trip with them into the days and weeks afterward.

- Work projects can sometimes come with disappointments, and there is often a lot of waiting around on a jobsite. This can be especially true when an eager group of students is given a task that was meant to last all morning or all day, and they complete it in just a few hours. Often jobsite coordinators have to scramble to get a job ready or must get the supplies that are needed for the next stage of a project before work can continue. More often than not, equipment breaks down or doesn't work at all, and everyone must wait until it is fixed or a new piece of equipment arrives. This can cause anxiety for students, who may feel as if their time is being wasted if they are not constantly working on a jobsite. They may want to move on to another job or create some work that they can do to keep busy. Here are some suggestions on how to handle this kind of situation:
  — Begin well. Before leaving for a work trip, I always tell students the best piece of advice that I was ever given on a mission trip: "The most important job on the jobsite is the one you've just been

given."[4] If you are asked to sweep the floor, that is an important task, because the area needs to be cleaned of debris before people can walk around the site safely or before a level floor covering can be installed. One of my favorite jobs to do during a construction project is to take the big magnet-on-a-stick around the site and pick up errant nails. If I find a student who feels bored or underutilized, I will hand him or her the magnet and demonstrate the joy of seeing nails magically emerge out of sawdust!

— Downtime on a jobsite can be a good time to practice reflection. Gather some students together and ask them how things are going. Help them process their feelings about having to wait around. Encourage them to think about ways they can usefully occupy their time.

— Build relationships. The times when work isn't being done on a mission trip are great opportunities to get to know the older, often retired volunteers and learn their life stories. Get to know the people in the neighborhood, and learn about their culture. One trip leader I know, a pharmacy professor at Ohio Northern, knows all the best places to get a cup of coffee and a donut

---

4 Rev. Jan "PJ" Yandell gave this advice to a group of United Methodist elders and our bishop during a work mission trip once, and it has become an important mantra for me in both mission work and my own daily work.

in Jackson and has cultivated a relationship with the proprietors of a crawdad boil, who willingly supply the students an abundance of the spicy "mud bugs" whenever they are in town. Such relationships build authenticity into the work that is being done and put a human face to the tasks that students are asked to perform.

— Practice being a non-anxious presence. A lull in the action on a work trip can cause students to feel anxious, but unless there is a safety issue that demands immediate attention, there is no need for you to also be anxious. Seeing that their chaplain or campus minister is not bothered by a lack of work to do can help students cope with the downtime and may lead them to model non-anxiety to their fellow students.

— Practice one of the other disciplines. Pull out this book, or reach into your knowledge about spiritual disciplines, and use the opportunity you have to teach students about a new practice. Lead the students in contemplative prayer or organize a group to offer prayer to the other workers on the jobsite. Have someone read aloud from Scripture or from an inspirational text. Do a session of Lectio Divina.

• Mission trips are a great time to talk about authentic community. In a world where community exists primarily in superficial quantities, it is important for collegiate ministry leaders to have conversations with their students about what it means to live in a true loving, caring Christian community. It may be helpful to write a community "rule" for the time the group is together, encouraging participants to take part in the writing of the rule and asking them to commit to living by it throughout the entire work trip. You might even write your group's rule as part of the preparatory sessions leading up to the trip and encourage living by the rule before, during, and after the trip.

- One-off events, such as single days of service or short-term projects, can also be fertile soil for spiritual reflection. Here is a quick way to reflect on a short service opportunity with your group:
  — Form a circle and have everyone think for a moment about how they feel right now.
  — Have each person in turn give a one-word response to the question, "How are you feeling?" No explanations are necessary, just one word.
  — Next, have each participant turn to one person beside him or her, and allow the pairs a couple of minutes to discuss their one-word responses. Both people in a pair should have time to explain their one-word response.
  — Have each pair find another pair and allow a few more minutes for the new groups of four to share their reflections.
  — Bring everyone back to the circle again and allow time for people to give a few short words about

what their groups discussed. Look for common themes and write them on a large sheet of paper or a dry-erase board.

— If the group is reluctant to share, or especially if it is the first time the group has come together, it may be helpful to have a few prompts ready for discussion, such as "Where did you see God at work today?"

— You may wish to end your time of reflection with a prayer, either shared communally with each participant speaking his or her prayers aloud, or with one person praying on behalf of the whole group, offering prayers based on the common themes that have been identified. The comfort level of every group will be different, and you will be able to discern the best way to conclude the group reflection.

• It is important in reflecting on service experiences to allow space for both personal and group reflections. Introverted people may need some time and space to think about their feelings before they can share with a larger group. On the other hand, extroverts will want to spend some time sharing with the group, especially if there is an opportunity to provide feedback and encouragement to one another.

However you choose to implement service within your ministry setting, it is important to see this as an opportunity to participate in a spiritual discipline. When placed within the context of being a means of grace or a vehicle for spiritual growth, service can take on new depths of meaning for your students. Deep reflection on the meaning behind service can also have a profound impact on your own spiritual life. Do not forget that you are also growing in your faith just as much as your students, and every opportunity you provide for their growth can also be an opportunity for your own growth.

Fun Fact: Habitat for Humanity was founded in 1976 by Millard and Linda Fuller. Since that time, the organization has helped build adequate housing for nearly ten million people.

Questions for Reflection

1. In your experience, what is the best way to help students fully participate in service rather than being only voyeurs or spectators, helping "those people"?
2. What kinds of spiritual preparations are necessary before offering service?
3. How might you talk about the difference between ministry with and ministry for others?
4. Often when a group goes on a retreat or mission/ service trip of some kind, the participants come back bonded in new ways. This can mean that those "left behind" are now outsiders, or the total group has been fractured, with negative effects. What are some ways to prevent this?

6 SPIRITUAL DIRECTION

"Spiritual direction," wrote Henri Nouwen in 1981, "is direction given to people in their relationship with God."[1] This practice has its roots in the monastic practice of the formation of postulants for life membership in a covenanted community. Men and women who wish to join a monastic order are assigned mentors, with whom they meet regularly for reflection, accountability, and sometimes correction or discipline. The role of the "spiritual director" in the monastic context is that of helping a person become conformed to the practices and charism of a particular religious community. Spiritual directors in the Jesuit community, for instance, are tasked with helping guide retreats for those who wish to participate in the Ignatian Spiritual Exercises. In other settings a spiritual director works more generally to help individuals in the development of their faith. Spiritual directors can be attached to local congregations or may have their own private practices, much like a therapist. Unlike a therapist, however, spiritual directors concentrate their work on the spiritual life of their directees, rather than their emotional or mental health—although

---

1   Henri J. M. Nouwen, "Spiritual Direction," *Worship 55*, no. 5 (1981): 399.

concern for these aspects of a person's life certainly make their way into spiritual direction, and most spiritual directors will also refer their directees to trained psychological professionals if the need arises.

A student walked into our office one day and wanted to speak with the chaplain.[2] Since I was in, my assistant sent him straight through. After a pleasant greeting, we sat down, and I said, "So, what brings you here today?" An hour later, I had heard much of his life story, along with all of the troubles he was experiencing at school. He had just broken up with his girlfriend, and he wasn't sure he was going to pass a class that was really important for his major. He wanted advice on what to do next. "Well," I said, "if you're looking for advice, you've come to the wrong place. That's not what I do. But what I can do is sit here with you and ask you some questions, and then listen to your story, and then ask a few more questions, and then listen some more, and then we'll see where we are. Why don't we set up a time to meet next week so you can talk some more and I can listen and ask more questions?"

After a few meetings with a student such as the one I just described, I can usually help them discern what steps they might need to take to go further in their relationship with God. The question I ask at the beginning of every spiritual direction session with a student is the same one that John Wesley's early band and class leaders asked: "How is

---

2   This is a composite portrait of the types of students I see in my practice of spiritual direction. It is not meant to portray a specific student.

it with your soul?" This question can lead a person in many directions and is a good way to check in with someone at the beginning of a session. A good spiritual director will allow the directee enough space and time to answer that first question, even if that is the only question that they get to during the entire hour they are in the office. The time spent between a director and directee is really time spent between the directee and God, with the director present as a companion—and sometimes a guide, when the directee doesn't know where to go next.

Introducing Spiritual Direction

There are two schools of thought on what makes one a spiritual director. The first is that a person is considered a spiritual director when he or she is asked by someone else to fulfill that role. In this case, the director is usually a well-respected, older member of the community, or perhaps a person, like a director of novices, whom the community chooses to fill this role. The second school of thought has come on the scene more recently, especially with the advent of spiritual directors in stand-alone practices: that a person must go through some form of intense training, usually involving both classwork and supervised clinical work, more akin to a clinical pastoral education course than to a monastic community. My own opinion on the matter is that this is a both-and situation and that people come to spiritual direction via many pathways, all of which can enrich the practice within the wider context of the church. For some, formal training in the techniques, ethical principles, and theories of spiritual direction and formation may be very important. For others, simply being present as a listening ear or as an *anam cara* ("spirit friend") is all that is required. The best approach is probably a mixture of the two; a call to spiritual direction through a friend who is seeking someone to be a companion for the journey of faith might lead one to seek to study spiritual direction in a more formal way, or the desire to obtain licensure or recognition as a professional in the field might lead to deep spiritual companionship with one's clients or directees.

I prefer to see my role as a campus chaplain from the perspective of being a spiritual director. I am not a pastor, in the sense that I do not have a congregation of members with whom I am in long-term relationship as a spiritual leader. In fact, my "congregation" leaves for three months out of the year and leaves for good in four years—indeed, I get a partially new congregation every year. I am also not a member of the faculty, since my primary responsibilities are not in teaching or doing research but in providing direct spiritual services to students. Neither fish nor fowl, those of us who are in collegiate ministry are called to work with people in a very specific group (college students), while not having the *imprimatur* of faculty status. As spiritual directors to the community, collegiate ministers are in the community but not necessarily of the community. They can act as neutral parties, often brokering peace and cooperation between disparate factions, or as impartial witnesses to the pain and struggles of students, faculty, and staff alike. The collegiate minister as spiritual director is responsible to reach out to all members of the community, not merely those with whom he or she shares an affinity, and of being a non-anxious presence on the campus during times of stress. This means that we collegiate ministers have the privilege of being approachable and that people will share very intimate details about their lives with us. This is not something to be taken lightly, nor should it be abused for personal gain.

Individual spiritual direction can take many forms. Most often it can take the form of a conversation in which a person who is seeking direction brings whatever issues, concerns, or topics that are on his or her mind, and the director listens carefully. The process of listening can have a profound effect on an individual, and as is the case in certain therapeutic processes, it can be helpful for the director to echo back what is heard, so that the directee can hear his or her own words in a different voice. This usually enables the directee to realize something in his or her words that he or she hadn't noticed before. That can then be a good starting point for direction. For instance, a session might go something like this:

> Director: Tell me, how is it with your soul?
>
> Directee: Not good. It's been a hectic week, and I just haven't had time to pray.
>
> Director: So, in the midst of a hectic time in your life, you've not been able to find the time to pray?
>
> Directee: Well, maybe it's not so much that I haven't been able to find the time to pray, as I just haven't made prayer a priority. I have plenty of time to do other things, like watch TV or play video games,

but I just can't seem to prioritize prayer in my daily routine.

Director: Sometimes, we prioritize the things that give us some perceived benefit. Would you say that doing other activities, like watching TV or playing video games, gives you something that prayer does not?

Directee: Yeah, I'd say that TV and video games relax me. They make me forget about my troubles.

Director: What about prayer? Does it have the same effect?

Directee: Not really. Actually, thinking about praying causes even more stress!

Director: Why do you think that is?

Directee: I don't know. Probably because I'm afraid I won't get the words right, or that my problems are too small to bother God with.

Director: But if they're problems for you, why wouldn't God want to hear about them?

Directee: I haven't thought about it that way . . . Does God really care about my small problems?

Director: Are they small problems?

Directee: Not really. They're pretty big—to me at least.

Director: I wonder, then, if they might be seen as big enough to take to God too.

Directee: Yeah, I guess so. But I still worry that I won't get the words right.

This then gives the director an opportunity to explore what the directee thinks "the right words" are, and then having him or her unpack what that means. Through asking questions and making observations based on the directee's own words, the director can help the directee dig deeper into the spiritual issues those words present and develop an understanding and practice that will enable him or her to turn those issues into opportunities for spiritual growth.

In a typical church or private practice of spiritual direction, a director may meet about once per month, or even once a quarter, with a directee. In college settings, directors may find that they need to meet more frequently, at least at first, with their students. I find it effective to meet with a student once a week for about a month, and then every other week, and then once a month. Often, students will only come in for one to three sessions and will not return. This used to worry me because I thought maybe I had done something to offend them, or perhaps my direction wasn't being very helpful. It wasn't until I had several conversations with colleagues in similar ministry settings that I found out this is normal. Sometimes students will show up for only one session, and that will be enough for them to get back on track with their spiritual formation—or at least they perceive it to be so. Then, sometimes, after not seeing someone for months, that individual will suddenly turn up at the door, asking for another meeting.

These kinds of patterns just seem to come with the territory in collegiate ministry, and it is far better to accept them as part of the pattern of development for emerging adults than to try to force something on students for which they are not ready. I have found that students will appear and disappear, and then reappear again when they need direction, and that a big part of my job is maintaining an open door through which they can walk when they are ready.

Spiritual direction does not have to be just a one-on-one spiritual practice. In fact, thanks to the work of scholars such as Sr. Rosemary Dougherty, the concept of spiritual direction can also be utilized by groups of people who wish to grow together in their faith.[3] Groups for spiritual direction can be used to help participants open themselves up to new ways of seeing their personal issues and struggles, in light of the sharing of others.

On a warm fall Sunday evening in 2013, a group of nine first-year college students gathered in the multi-faith room in the chapel at Ohio Northern University. They were there to take part in a group called Merge, which had been billed as an opportunity to participate in something called "group spiritual direction." Their chaplain, who was leading the group, had already met each member of the new group individually, since they had to undergo an interview process to become part of the group, but they had never met one another before that night. In the history of awkward meetings, that gathering had to be near the top of the list or should at least have been awarded an honorable mention for "Most Awkward Meeting of College Students in the History of Ever."

I was the chaplain leading that group of students, and Merge was born out of my participation in the doctor of ministry program in spiritual formation at Garrett-Evangelical

---

3   See Rosemary Daugherty, *Group Spiritual Direction for Community Discernment* (Mahwah, NJ: Paulist Press, 1995).

Theological Seminary. My studies at Garrett had actually led directly to my presence in that awkward room that night, since my experience in the program had led me to discern a call to college chaplaincy. Sitting in the office of my advisor, Dr. Dwight Judy, I had gone into a long description of the kind of ministry I would love to be doing with young adults, to which Dwight responded, "If you want to work with young adults, why aren't you on a college campus?" That off-the-cuff remark (Dwight swore to me later that he didn't remember saying it) sparked an interest in collegiate ministry that led to my being hired as the university chaplain at Ohio Northern in 2012 and to the creation of Merge the following year.

As I write this, the last of the original Merge members are in their final semester of college. The bittersweet moment of their commencement into the so-called real world is a reminder of the all too short amount of time that collegiate ministers have with their students, but the large impact they can make in that time (and that their students make on their lives, as well). Over the past few years, the members of that original cohort have become leaders within Merge and within the campus community at large. They are a diverse group of individuals who are joined together in their commitment to finding the "quiet center" of their lives through silence, reflection, and conversation with others in the context of spiritual direction. It is my hope that they will emerge from this experience as trained leaders who will be able to implement the lessons they have learned in Merge in their churches and communities in the future.

The Merge model for group spiritual direction consists of eight movements, and meetings generally last for an hour and a half. These are the movements:

1. **Business (10 minutes):** During this time the group discusses any upcoming events (such as retreats or away days), and student leaders make any reminders that need to be brought up to the group.

2. **Silence (5 minutes):** Using a timer with a pleasant-sounding alarm (such as a bell or singing bowl), the group spends time in silence as a way of centering themselves.

3. **"Third Thing" (5-10 minutes):** According to Parker Palmer a "third thing" can be "a poem, a story, a piece of music, or a work of art" that allows the group to look at topics that may be difficult or uncomfortable.[4]

4. **Silence (5 minutes):** The second silence allows the group members the time and space to reflect on the Third Thing.

5. **Paired Conversations (15-20 minutes):** A large portion of the group's time is spent in conversation pairs, where participants talk about their reflections on the Third Thing, or on any topic that comes to mind. Time should be shared equally between partners, with one person speaking and the other listening without judgment and without trying to "fix" the speaker's problems or issues. Partners then switch

---

4   Parker J. Palmer, *A Hidden Wholeness: The Journey Toward an Undivided Life* (San Francisco: Jossey-Bass, 2004).

roles, and the person who has been listening will be the speaker. Partners are encouraged to ask open-ended questions and not try to change the speaker's mind or fix any problems he or she may present, but to merely offer questions and observations.[5]

6. **Group Conversation (10 minutes):** Pairs come back together in the large group, where reflections and thoughts about the Third Thing are shared by all those who feel comfortable. Each person is invited to share only his or her own reflections. At this point the facilitator for that week (usually one of the older, more experienced members of the group) may ask questions or offer observations about what has been said. As before, the goal is not to "fix" anyone or any situation but to clarify.

7. **Creative Expressions (15-20 minutes):** Students are invited to reflect on what they have seen, heard, and experienced during the session in a creative format. Each week, the medium for creative expressions changes. Some examples include: clay, paint, colored pencils, Play-Doh, chalk, and free writing. The creative expressions are meant to serve as a reminder of that week's session, which participants may take with them when they leave. Some students

---

5   The source of this pattern is an article by Jane Vennard, a respected spiritual director and writer in the field of spiritual formation. See her article titled "The Compassionate Observer: An Experiential Model for Formation," in *Presence: The Journal of Spiritual Directors International* 4, no. 3 (September 1998): 24-33.

have decorated their dorm rooms or apartments entirely in creative expression projects from Merge!

8. **Fellowship (10 minutes):** The last ten minutes of the session are reserved for fellowship, which usually involves sharing food. During this time, students interact freely with one another and build long-lasting friendships with other group members.

Guiding Principles and Group Covenant

Groups organized for the purpose of spiritual direction must be organized by some kind of guiding principles. For Merge, the most important guiding principle is confidentiality. Each year the group's leaders remind students that what is said in Merge must be kept confidential. The only time this principle is broken is when the group believes that a person may be a danger to himself or herself or to others, at which point they usually alert campus resources such as the chaplain or office of student affairs. Another guiding principle of Merge is that once an atmosphere of confidentiality has been established, everyone is encouraged to share freely—not withholding or feeling embarrassed to share their thoughts. Of course, everyone is also allowed to keep some things private, and so the principle of privacy is also important. Our third guiding principle is that of self-agency. Each person in the group is ultimately responsible for his or her own spiritual formation, and as such has the power to remain the same or make changes. No other person can force change, try to "fix" another member of the group, or take responsibility for the actions or reactions of others. It is important in group spiritual direction that everyone understand that even though the group has a shared purpose of creating an environment of spiritual growth, individuals grow differently, at different paces, and to different ends. What is right and good and true for one member of the group may be destructive for another, and all members' perspectives should be respected, even if we don't always agree.

Each group that is organized for spiritual direction must, in addition to the guiding principles already mentioned, create their own group covenant for the time they are together. The inaugural Merge participants created their own covenant, and each year this is revisited, since the group essentially changes in character as each class graduates and is replaced by a new incoming class of students. Among the typical items that are included in a group covenant might be these:

- We will start and end on time, to respect people's busy lives and commitments.
- We will not use our cell phones during group sessions, unless we are using a phone as a music player for a Third Thing.
- We will respect the space where we meet and clean it when we are done.
- We will respect one another and will not look down on someone because of something he or she shares while in the group. (The first group of Merge participants called this the "Don't be judgy" rule.)

- We will welcome newcomers to the group and will not create an environment that promotes an "in group" and an "out group." Returning members will go out of their way to pair up with new members in the beginning of the year to get to know them and help them feel welcome.

Group covenants will be as unique as each group that gathers for spiritual direction and may change or evolve over time. It is important for group members to be clear with one another what is expected of them as participants in group spiritual direction. It may also be helpful to develop a plan for what happens if a person breaks the covenant. Will there be some kind of consequence? Who will speak with group members who do not abide by the covenant, and what corrective actions can be taken to help them understand the purpose behind the covenant? How can a person appropriately make amends with either the group or an individual who is hurt by the breaking of covenant? Most important, groups will want to take a graceful approach, not being too harsh, and remembering that even the breaking of covenant (and the reconciliation

Fun Fact: Spiritual Directors International is an organization that "serves and supports the ministry and service of spiritual direction." Their website, www.sdiworld.org, is a great place to find resources on spiritual direction. They also have a spiritual director locator that can help you find a spiritual director in your area.

that can happen afterward) can lead to individual and collective spiritual formation.

Whether individually or with a group, spiritual direction can be a powerful tool for collegiate ministers who wish to help students with their spiritual formation. While the typical tools of campus ministry—fellowship events, Bible studies, retreats, and the like—can be helpful for discipleship, spiritual direction can add another dimension to our work, one that calls students into a deeper conversation with each other, with mentors and guides, and with God.

Questions for Reflection

1. If you have experienced spiritual direction yourself, what was it like? Do you still continue to receive spiritual direction? If not, what caused you to stop going?

2. What might spiritual direction look like in your context? Of the types of spiritual direction listed in this chapter, to which one would your community be most receptive?

3. If you were to start a group for spiritual direction, what kind of covenant would you need to set up for the group?

4. How would your collegiate ministry be able to help students cope with the issues that may arise within them as they explore spiritual direction?

7 PILGRIMAGE

From its earliest days, Christianity has been a religion steeped in pilgrimage. Early Christians worshipped at the martyrdom sites of their saints, and places associated with Christ and the apostles were seen as having special significance and power. Thus, pilgrimages from across the Roman world to the Holy Land were common for those who could afford them. For those who could not, a short pilgrimage to a local holy site would have to suffice. This practice hit its peak during the Middle Ages, particularly as the scourge of bubonic plague ravaged Europe.[1] Pilgrimages such as the Camino de Santiago (Way of St. James) in Spain and the Pilgrim's Way from Winchester to Canterbury in England became byways that pilgrims frequently traveled in search of God's favor. Services such as hostels, guesthouses, taverns, and smaller shrines or churches dedicated to minor saints sprang up along such routes, leading to a burgeoning pilgrimage industry by the late Middle Ages. Benedictine practice and spirituality has been deeply influenced by the need to provide hospitality

---

1   Justo L. Gonzalez, *The Story of Christianity*, vol. 1, *The Early Church to the Dawn of the Reformation* (San Francisco: Harper Collins, 1984), 328.

to guests who are on pilgrimage—a practice which will be further explored in chapter 9.

Rev. Dr. Jeremiah Gibbs, chaplain at the University of Indianapolis, a United Methodist–related institution, has begun a practice of pilgrimage with students and faculty during their short spring term every other May. Approximately twenty-four students and faculty embarked on a pilgrimage on the Camino de Santiago in 2017, following the ancient Camino Frances for about 165 kilometers over the course of three weeks. Preparation for the pilgrimage began more than a year before, after the first group of student pilgrims returned from their first trip. Jeremiah developed a series of preparatory meetings, during which those who were going on the camino prepared mentally, physically, and spiritually for the arduous journey. Over the course of five meetings spread throughout the spring semester, participants went on practice hikes to try out their gear and get themselves into the mind-set needed for walking long distances. They also participated in readings and group discussions about the concept of pilgrimage, and specifically about the camino. During the most recent camino, Gibbs partnered with the honors college at UIndy. Students in that program who participated in the camino did additional readings on medieval history, culture, and religion.

When I asked Gibbs to tell me about the impact of the camino on his students, he replied, "There were a number of students, particularly those from the honors program, who had never spoken openly about their faith before. After being exposed to talking about faith for three straight weeks, it was like a switch had been flipped, and they were suddenly comfortable with 'religion talk' now." He also noted that the camino brought together Catholic and Protestant students who had not previously worshipped together on campus. Due to the low number of Protestant churches along the route of the camino, the students tended to all go together to the local Catholic churches for the various "pilgrim masses" that took place. This led to productive conversations between Protestant and Catholic students about the differences and similarities of their Christian traditions. As a result, Gibbs noted that worship in both the campus chapel program and the Catholic student organization on campus have been enriched in the year following the camino, as students who partook of the pilgrimage have returned to become leaders in their respective communities.[2]

Introducing Pilgrimage

The Benedictine movement was in part a response to the collapse of the Roman Empire, along with its superior system of roads, wall, and protective forts that had been scattered throughout Europe. With the fall of the empire, travelers to holy sites no longer enjoyed the *pax Romana* that once kept citizens of the empire subject to the laws of Rome and therefore safe wherever they went. Thus, pilgrims would frequently stop at monasteries along their pilgrimage route, because these communities of monks were seen as safe places for guests.

---

2   Interview with Rev. Dr. Jeremiah Gibbs, September 13, 2017.

Tips for Starting a Practice of Pilgrimage

Dr. Gibbs offers several tips for getting started with pilgrimage on a college campus:

1. Do your homework. Connect with groups online, such as the American Pilgrims on the Camino (APOC), who have resources and firsthand knowledge of the pilgrimage route you will be taking. If possible, try to take the pilgrimage, or at least part of it, in advance of taking a group of students. See if you can go along with a group of experienced pilgrims.

2. Work with colleagues on campus. Partnerships such as the one between the chapel and the honors college at the University of Indianapolis can be fruitful and lead to a richer experience for all involved.

3. Work out and be able to articulate why pilgrimage is important. Read books, such as those listed in the resources section of this book, that will ground you firmly in a historical and theological understanding of pilgrimage.

4. Don't oversell the pilgrimage or ramp up students' expectations. Dr. Gibbs noted that he had spoken of "miracles" and messages from God. As a result, the students thought that more was going to happen and that the change within them was going to be dramatic. "The change that's happening in people is much more subtle, but not less important," Gibbs said. "The students who have done this still talk about this as one of the most important parts

of their spiritual life. They can point to ways that their spirituality changed, and they talk about this experience as helping them to learn what it means to slow down."

Of course, not every collegiate ministry will be able to afford or pull off such a pilgrimage. Raising the funds for airfare to Europe and then having enough money to backpack from place to place for three weeks may not be something that can be accomplished right away. It may be possible, however, to plan a pilgrimage to a closer destination. A trip to a local church or monastery, in which part or all of the trip is done on foot, can be just as transformational for students who have never experienced pilgrimage before. A retreat at a nearby United Methodist camp can be a short-term kind of pilgrimage. One group on our campus has returned to the same Franciscan retreat center twice a year for the last several years. As the students have come to love that place and the sisters who live there, they have come to see their retreat experiences as a kind of pilgrimage to a place that has become holy to them simply through repeated visits. Another group went on retreat to Maria Stein, Ohio, and visited the relic chapel in the church there, which contains more than a thousand Christian relics.[3] Spending time in the relic chapel, reading about the various saints and holy sites from which the relics came, became a holy experience, even for those participants for whom the collection of relics is not part of their church tradition. One Lutheran participant was

---

3   See the shrine's website at http://www.mariasteinshrine.org/.

awed by the historical significance of the relics and said that being there made her feel part of the "great cloud of witnesses" of the church. (See Hebrews 12:1.)

The college experience itself can be a kind of pilgrimage experience. The typical college student who lives on campus must often move far away from home, or relatively so, leaving behind family, friends, and familiar surroundings. While on campus, students are exposed to challenges, new learning opportunities, and a gathering of strangers who come together in the end as a community. In the best of circumstances they are challenged in their assumptions about their faith and come through those challenges having experienced spiritual growth. When they leave college, whether they return home or not, they are changed in significant ways and will retain the lessons they learned for the rest of their lives. The college experience is the closest thing that many North American young people have to the liminal experiences of traditional rites of passage. With the articulation of the concept of emerging adulthood by Jeffrey Jensen Arnett and others, it is now widely held that adulthood is beginning later and that the years between the ages of eighteen and twenty-five are a time when young people are still developing into the adults they will become.[4] This is a great opportunity for collegiate ministers to be companions on the journey through the growth period of emerging adulthood, acting as mentors and guides along the way. Many of the

---

4   Jeffrey Jensen Arnett, "Emerging Adulthood: A Theory of Development from the Late Teens Through the Twenties," *American Psychologist* 55, no. 5 (May 2000): 469–80.

other practices in this book can be helpful tools for those who wish to engage in the model of collegiate ministry as pilgrimage, but here are some ideas for other ways pilgrimage could become part of your ministry:

1. Identify places on campus that are considered "holy" to the campus community. If you are on a private campus, the chapel or other worship space might be one such place. On some campuses, the sites of significant events in the history of the college might take on a kind of holiness for the community. One example of such a place would be the May 4 memorial on the campus of Kent State University, where four students were shot and killed on May 4, 1970, as they protested the war in Vietnam.[5] Sites with such historical or religious significance often take on the air of places of pilgrimage, especially during times of tragedy.

2. Encourage student groups to establish traditions of going on retreats. One group at Ohio Northern goes to "Indy CC" every year over the Christmas break. This national gathering of students who are involved with Cru has become a kind of pilgrimage for the students, as they return each year and then pass on the excitement of going on the retreat to incoming students.

---

5   See "May 4 Memorial (Kent State University)" on the Kent State University website, at http://www.library.kent.edu/special-collections -and-archives/may-4-memorial-kent-state-university.

3. Utilize opportunities when you will be near significant sites with student groups to visit those sites as a group experience. During a Habitat for Humanity work trip to Birmingham, Alabama, I had the honor of introducing a group of students to Kelly Ingram Park and the surrounding neighborhood. We spent the afternoon walking around the park, taking in the monuments and sculptures that memorialized the sacrifices of those who participated in the civil rights movement, and then visited the Sixteenth Street Baptist Church, site of a bombing that took the lives of four girls as they met for Sunday school on September 15, 1963. Students later counted the trip to the Civil Rights District as one of the highlights of their trip.

4. Invite students who have been on significant pilgrimage journeys, such as the camino, to speak with student groups, or as part of your worship experience. Invite them to reflect on how their practice of pilgrimage has changed or affected their college experience.

The practice of pilgrimage can greatly enrich collegiate ministry. You will find that the students with whom you spend time while on pilgrimage will become some of your most active participants in ministry and will often become lifelong friends and colleagues after they have graduated. Pilgrimage can also have a profound effect on you as a collegiate minister, as you will grow from the challenges and moments of enlightenment while walking "the Way."

Questions for Reflection

1. Are there any pilgrimage sites located near your ministry site? How might you go about exploring the option of visiting one or more of these sites?

2. What are the "holy sites" on your campus? What do people do there? How could you incorporate the pilgrimages to these sites in your ministry?

Fun Fact: Many ancient Celtic saints practiced what was known as *peregrination*, or a wandering away from one's homeland in order to "find the place of one's resurrection." This literally meant a pilgrimage to a place where one would live out the rest of one's life, die, and thus be resurrected in the last days.

3. If you could take a group of students from your ministry setting on any pilgrimage journey in the world, what would it be? What kinds of logistical issues would need to be addressed in order for your group to go to that place? Begin sketching out a plan for a pilgrimage.

4. How do you respond to the idea that the college experience is like a pilgrimage? How might this image be useful to the students in your ministry?

8 INTENTIONAL COMMUNITY

In his *Rule*, Saint Benedict wrote, "We intend to establish a school for the Lord's service. In drawing up its regulations, we hope to set down nothing harsh, nothing burdensome. The good of all concerned, however, may prompt us to a little strictness in order to amend faults and to safeguard love."[1] Many communities since Benedict's time have based their rules of life on his original *Rule*, and his words are often read aloud during meal gatherings in many Benedictine communities, as a way of keeping the foundation of their order at the forefront of the minds of all community members. Benedict wrote, "It is called a rule because it regulates the lives of those who obey it."[2] While religious communities based on a common rule have existed for centuries, a new monastic movement emerged in the latter part of the twentieth century, which called for communities to live lives guided by twelve "marks":

1) Relocation to the abandoned places of Empire.

2) Sharing economic resources with fellow community members and the needy among us.

3) Hospitality to the stranger.

---

1   Fry, *The Rule of St. Benedict in English,* 18–19 (see intro., n. 2).
2   Fry, 20.

4) Lament for racial divisions within the church and our communities combined with the active pursuit of a just reconciliation.

5) Humble submission to Christ's body, the church.

6) Intentional formation in the way of Christ and the rule of the community along the lines of the old novitiate.

7) Nurturing common life among members of intentional community.

8) Support for celibate singles alongside monogamous married couples and their children.

9) Geographical proximity to community members who share a common rule of life.

10) Care for the plot of God's earth given to us along with support of our local economies.

11) Peacemaking in the midst of violence and conflict resolution within communities along the lines of Matthew 18.

12) Commitment to a disciplined contemplative life.[3]

Located in upstate South Carolina, Greenville is the home of Furman University. Among the campus ministries serving Furman is the Mere Christianity Forum. Under the direction of Rev. Rimes McElveen, the Mere Christianity Forum is home to an intentional community of college students known as Vista House. Vista House began as an experiment in intentional community in 2003. Students in the founding group were residents of the Mere Christianity Forum's

---

3   Josh Andersen, "The 12 Marks of a New Monasticism," *Sojourners,* January 2007, https://sojo.net/magazine/january-2007/12-marks -new-monasticism.

housing units who desired to form a community where they could explore deep questions of their faith together. Rather than simply renting rooms from the campus ministry and existing in a landlord-tenant relationship, the residents sought to integrate the work of the campus ministry and the intentional community in ways that would benefit both.

As Reverend McElveen put it, "We don't take ourselves too seriously. . . . We're not the same thing as a monastic community . . . or even a new monastic community. But, we are a people who are bound by a covenant that we've made together."[4] The community of Vista House is structured so that leadership and responsibilities are shared on a rotational basis. Everyone pitches in, including Reverend McElveen himself. Daily prayer is held every morning, which is open to members of the community and guests. Every Wednesday, dinner is prepared and served by the students in the community. McElveen says that the dinners follow an "open-table/closed-table" pattern. Every other week the meal is for members of the Vista House community only. During these meals, the community attends to its business and frequently revisits the covenant they made at the beginning of the year to remind themselves of their rule of life. On the opposite weeks the meal is open to anyone who wishes to attend. At these open-table meals a professor or staff member of the university is usually invited to share something about his or her work or passion, and discussion is encouraged. The community also holds regular "tomfoolery" events for socializing and letting off steam.

---

4   Rimes McElveen, interview with author, September 15, 2017.

The Vista House program has also led to the creation of the "Servant Scholars" program in the summer. During the summer, students who are accepted as servant scholars live onsite in community at Vista House and serve as interns at local nonprofit agencies. The primary theme of this summer experience is vocational discernment, and members of the Servant Scholars community participate in common readings, writing assignments, and discussion.

What Makes Community Intentional?

College life is lived in community, and students are confronted daily with the realities of having to share space with others. Simple tasks, such as taking a shower, brushing one's teeth, doing laundry, and even eating meals are all regularly interrupted by encounters with others. Standing in lines and waiting one's turn is a large part of communal life on most campuses. But what makes a community *intentional* rather than just accidental? What is the difference between a group of people thrust together by the happenstance of a housing lottery and those who choose to live with intentionality?

Rimes McElveen offered his thoughts: "To me, intentional Christian community is a kind of plausibility structure." In such a structure, meaning-making occurs within a specific shared framework of beliefs, cultural norms, and practices. Thus, a community like Vista House is intentional insofar as its members agree to structure their lives with a common purpose in mind and abide by a shared rule that governs their life together. "The name Vista," McElveen said, "hearkens to an alternative vision of what community can look like on a university campus." Thus, the intentionality of that particular community is defined by a shared goal to model for others how Christians may live in unity with one another. Members of Vista House's community do not necessarily come from the same Christian traditions, but they have chosen to show others how Christians with different perspectives may work together for the common good. Thus, their rules and covenant are structured in a way that encourage interaction with one another alongside interaction with the wider campus community, in order to live out what they believe, which is that Christians can gain more from cooperating with one another than they can from remaining divided.

If you plan to begin an intentional community on your campus, you would be wise to remember the *intentionality* that is inherent in such an enterprise. Without a common rule or covenant, those who live together merely share a living space. With intentionality, a community and shared life can emerge. Here are some points to consider when starting an intentional community:

1. Is this something your students want? Is there a desire for intentional community on your campus or within your ministry? It could be difficult to begin and maintain an intentional community if there is active resistance, or worse yet, if there is simply no desire for such a ministry.

2. What are the housing regulations on the campus where you do ministry? If you are looking to start an

off-campus intentional community—say, at a Wesley Foundation site—it would be important to know if the college or university restricts off-campus living in some way. Many larger institutions require first-year students to live on campus. Many smaller institutions and, increasingly, larger institutions as well, now require students to live on campus for their first two or even three years. This will limit the population from which you will be able to draw your community members.

3. Are there housing restrictions or zoning issues you need to explore with the community in which your building is located? If your building was originally a church, it may not be zoned for housing, and you may need to work with your town or city zoning office to get the building up to code.

4. What kind of facilities do you have, and what improvements need to be made before you explore the possibility of an intentional community? Some campus ministry facilities are located in former or current church buildings and were not set up to house students. Others were created with housing in mind but were constructed during a time when it was the norm to have students rent individual living spaces, thus leaving no space for the interaction needed in an intentional community.

5. How will your efforts be funded? There are some grants available for starting pilot projects, especially when the intentional community you have in mind

has a specific theme, such as vocational discernment. Sustainable funding must be secured for an intentional community to survive in the long term. Will you collect rent from the members of the community? Will fund-raising efforts be needed, and if so, how can your board get involved? Will you take the traditional monastic route and create some products or provide some services that would be of use to people outside the community that can help pay the bills? Some monastic communities make baked goods, candles, crafts, works of art, or even beer as a way of sustaining themselves. Having a brewery on-site might be a tough sell for your board of directors, but there may be some kind of good or service your community could provide, such as a coffeehouse, that would help pay the bills.

6. How will the community create a covenant by which they will agree to live, and how often will that covenant be revisited and revised? It may be a good idea to have a community retreat once a year before the beginning of the fall term, to bring in new members and revise the community covenant before another year begins.

7. What role will the campus minister, chaplain, or pastor play within the community? This may be flexible depending on the staff that are available from year to year, or there may be a fairly consistent and well-defined role for the collegiate minister. Reverend McElveen noted that the role closest to what he

fills in Vista House is that of abbot. There are times when he is called upon to settle disputes or offer spiritual guidance and care, but more often than not, he serves as a facilitator for community discussions and decisions.

However your community decides to structure itself, intentional community can be a powerful way to create a space for in-depth discipleship in your collegiate ministry. Of the practices that have been mentioned so far, this one is perhaps the most intense and brings with it the most potential for risk, but also the most potential for reward. An intentional community based out of your collegiate ministry can provide a ready-made group of well-trained, highly motivated student leaders who can serve as the basis for a growing ministry.

When intentional communities are at their best, they are highly invitational and hospitable in nature. Thus, students who are part of your intentional community can help to reach out to other students on campus who may not be quite ready to take on the full covenant of the community but who are intrigued by the kind of sharing and mutual care that can be expressed within an intentional

Fun Fact: Reba Place Fellowship is an intentional community based in Chicago and Evanston, Illinois. They describe their call as a community in this way: "*The calling of Reba Place Fellowship is to extend the mission of Jesus by being a community of love and discipleship and by nurturing other such communities as God gives us grace.*"

community. Over time, an intentional community that has a mission to undergird the work of the collegiate ministry as a whole can provide a strong base from which to operate on a college campus.

Questions for Reflection

1. Do you think an intentional community would be a burden or a blessing to your current ministry? What might have to change about the way you do things in your ministry setting if you were to implement an intentional community?
2. Who among your ministry leaders and participants would be most interested in living in an intentional community?
3. If you had all the resources to start an intentional community tomorrow—money, space for living and meeting, and willing participants—what might that community look like? What kind of covenant would your community have? What would its mission be?
4. Of the issues listed in this chapter, which ones do you not know enough about yet to make a decision about whether or not to have an intentional community as part of your ministry? Where might you begin to gather the information you would need to address those issues?

9 HOSPITALITY

In Saint Benedict's *Rule*, hospitality is a major concern for the members of the monastic community. In fact, Benedict wrote that when guests appear at the monastery, they "are to be welcomed as Christ, for he himself will say, 'I was a stranger and you welcomed me' (Matthew 25:35)." A bit further on in the *Rule*, Benedict wrote that all work should cease, and the superior (abbot) and all the monks should gather and greet a guest "by a bow of the head or by a complete prostration of the body," as one might greet Christ. The guest is invited to prayer with the community. Afterward, the abbot of the monastery should sit with the guest and have someone read the *Rule* aloud so that the guest is aware of what will be expected of him or her during his or her time in the monastery. Finally, the guest is treated to a meal. Because hospitality is so important in the *Rule*, Benedict wrote that "the superior may break his fast for the sake of a guest."[1] The ancient practice of welcoming guests is still practiced, to lesser or greater extent, by most monasteries today. At the Abbey of Gethsemani, for instance, guests are welcomed by the master of guests, who is a brother assigned the task of taking care of retreatants and

---

1   Fry, *The Rule of St. Benedict in English,* 73–74 (see intro., n. 2).

visitors. The master of guests also provides periodic talks for visitors on topics such as the monastic life or prayer practices. Guests at Gethsemani are not expected to pay a set fee for their room and board, although donations to the community are welcome. This is in keeping with the monastic tradition of offering hospitality to all, regardless of their ability to pay. Often, ancient monasteries were built along pilgrimage routes and offered refuge to poor travelers who sought a place to sleep and a warm meal while on the road. While some monasteries today do charge a fee for retreatants, most are open to offering space for those who cannot afford the set fees, or they offer a sliding scale of fees as a way to accommodate all.

David Glenn-Burns is the campus minister at Three-house: A Wesley Foundation at the University of Northern Iowa, located in Cedar Falls. He describes Threehouse as a place of hospitality just off the UNI campus, "a sacred and safe space where people can encounter 'the other.'" Three-house came about after a storm blew the roof off the Wesley Foundation building in 2009. At the time, Reverend Glenn-Burns noted, there was a discussion about whether or not to continue having a physical presence in the form of a building. There was some thought given to simply giving Dave a laptop and telling him to roam the campus, working with students. After some discussion, the board decided that the building, and particularly its location adjacent to the campus, was a strategic asset, since there were few churches in the area. Thus, Threehouse was born as a ministry of hospitality to the campus.

In an average week Threehouse will host more non-ministry-related groups than ministry-related groups. While the Wesley Foundation does have weekly worship and Bible study, they have also chosen to open their building to be used by a wide variety of campus and community groups. Reverend Glenn-Burns described one weekend where a burlesque-style drag show was held in the evening and a Bible study was held in the same space the next morning. Threehouse has opened its doors to the LGBTQ+ community on campus, the Black Student Union, the Shia Muslim student organization, and an improv group, among others. In one year, more than twelve thousand people utilized the building in one way or another. The Threehouse community sees the gift of their building as a way to offer hospitality to people with whom other churches or Christian organizations may not normally associate. In one instance Threehouse offered space to a group of Muslim women who were looking for a place where they could exercise in private. Reverend Glenn-Burns sees this as a way of transcending traditional boundaries, offering the love of Christ to everyone. Threehouse also prides itself on being a truly ecumenical ministry. Even though it is strongly related to The United Methodist Church, the ministry also has ties to Presbyterian and Episcopalian campus ministries. The "threeness" of the denominations represented, along with the "Threeness" of the Trinity, is part of where the name "Threehouse" comes from. The community also drew upon the work of sociologist Ray Oldenburg, who coined the term "third places" in advocating for more public spaces in urban environments where people can come together to interact.[2]

While offering their building as a hospitable space for the entire campus has many rewards and offers Threehouse an opportunity to witness to the love of God on their campus, it can also come with some drawbacks. Since outside events are not completely under the control of the Threehouse staff or board, building users can sometimes break rules or cause disturbances. The ministry has had to build good relations with the local police and with campus leaders in order to maintain peace and tranquility for all. "We are always working on our building use policy," Glenn-Burns noted, "and sometimes events bring up issues that we hadn't thought about before, so we have to make changes to the policy."[3] Such flexibility is necessary to make sharing a building with the wider community possible. Here are some things to think about if you have a space that you'd like to offer your campus in an effort to be more hospitable:

1. Make sure you have a strong and clearly worded building use policy, and ensure that groups wishing to utilize your facilities understand and acknowledge your policies. It is important that outside groups understand the appropriate boundaries that exist within a building and that property and people are treated respectfully.

---

2   See Project for Public Spaces, "Ray Oldenburg," PPS.org, December 31, 2008, https://www.pps.org/reference/roldenburg/.

3   David Glenn-Burns, interview with author, September 20, 2017.

2. It would be good to have a conversation early on to decide if the offering of your building is primarily an act of hospitality or is seen as a means of raising funds. Each of these can be valid uses of a building, but each will also come with different expectations about how the building may be used, who may use the building, and what kinds of boundaries need to be set up.

3. Have a clear understanding of why you are offering hospitality to the community. Hospitality is a spiritual discipline when it reflects the desire to share the love of Christ with others.

4. Be clear with your board, funders, and conference boards of higher education about the direction you are taking if you decide to offer your space as a place of hospitality. It will be important to know up front if your church constituents will have an objection to certain types of facility uses in order to prevent any misunderstandings down the road.

5. Make your contact with groups using your space as personal as possible. If you invited a guest into your home, you wouldn't have him or her fill out an online form, leave a key in a lock box, and then leave that guest to find things on his or her own. In the same way, guests in your ministry facility will appreciate it if you greet them personally, show them around, and answer any questions or concerns they may have in a timely manner.

For those like me, whose buildings are on campus and owned by the college or university, hospitality may mean offering space for many events outside of the purview of religious life. For instance, our chapel has seating for more than three hundred people, making it the third-largest space on campus, after our fieldhouse and performing arts center. As a result, we host many lectures, panel discussions, orientation sessions, and academic ceremonies throughout the year. We also have the advantage of being one of the few buildings on our campus that is not covered by the university's agreement with our food service provider. This means that many groups who want to provide their own food, rather than ordering from food services, will utilize our space. If you happen to be lucky enough to have a space—on campus of off—where students can get a "home-cooked" meal, a ministry of hospitality might be a good idea for you.

Fun Fact: The words *hospitality* and *hostility* both share the same Latin root word, meaning "guest," or "stranger." The way we approach those who are strangers to us can either lead to hospitality or hostility.

Beginning a ministry of hospitality can be a risky proposition. We in the church are used to having our sacred spaces "just so," and we do not often open them to outsiders. It may be that offering Threehouse-style accommodation to outside groups is not for you. It is better to figure that out now than to find out when the drag queens and the ladies' Bible study show up on the same night expecting to use the same space! Offering hospitality always comes with a price. After all, in monastic communities, the arrival of a guest means that everyone must stop what they are doing to see to the guest's needs. A true ministry of hospitality in a collegiate ministry setting will mean being willing to greet every visitor, no matter what the time, day, or season, with a hearty smile and a bow of respect, for it is not the visitor you are greeting but the living Christ himself.

Questions for Reflection

1. What potential does your current space offer for a ministry of hospitality? What are some of the limiting factors for you in starting this kind of ministry?
2. What groups on your campus might you be able to reach out to as potential building users? What natural partnerships already exist with those groups, or how could you cultivate relationships with them?
3. What objections might funders, board members, or church constituencies have to a hospitality ministry in your setting? How could you acknowledge and overcome those objections already, and what might you need to work on to alleviate other objections that would remain?
4. What relationships, such as with campus police or security teams, do you need to be cultivating in order to have an effective ministry of hospitality within a safe environment?
5. What are you willing to drop in order to focus more on hospitality?

THE LAST WORD: THIS IS NOT THE LAST WORD

I suppose the conclusion of a book should be the last word, but as I said in the beginning, "You are already the expert in what you do and in your context." The final word really belongs to you. What will you do with the concepts you've encountered and discussed while reading this book? In what ways could the spiritual disciplines described here change or enhance your ministry on college campuses? What are you most excited about implementing, and what scares you the most? The answers to these questions will lead you forward in becoming even more of an expert in the ministry to which God has called you.

As I stated in the introduction, this book is not meant to be read in isolation. I hope you have shared it along with way with your student leaders, members of your board, or faculty and staff advisers to your organizations on campus. If not, now is the time to start thinking about who would most benefit from reading about the practices you've just read about. Use the discussion questions to spark some creativity and dialogue in your ministry setting about the places where God might be calling you to go next.

When you do decide on a new spiritual discipline to introduce into your ministry context, you might want to fill in the following statements to help in your planning:

1. Name a spiritual discipline.
2. How will it be implemented in our context?
3. Who will be on the team doing the implementation?
4. What resources will the team need?
5. What existing community or campus partners can we bring in?
6. What is our goal?
7. What is our desired impact?
8. How does that goal fit within the stated mission and goals of our organization?
9. How will we know we have met our goal?
10. How will we continue to evaluate the implementation of this practice?

Open yourself up to new possibilities in ministry by introducing these practices, or others like them, into your collegiate ministry. As with all new ideas, give your practices time to develop, and be patient with yourself and the community in which you serve. Sometimes it takes a while for new practices to catch on. Sometimes only a small number of people will be attracted to the more intense spiritual disciplines. The measure of the success of implementing such practices may simply be that they exist within the larger framework of your ministry in order to provide some spiritual growth to a group of people who had not previously been reached by your ministry. That may be success enough. You will be amazed at the ways God can work through small groups practicing spiritual disciplines to reinvigorate your community.

Ora et labora!

RESOURCES

Communal Prayer (chapter 2)

Shane Claiborne, Jonathan Wilson-Hartgrove, and Enuma Okoro, *Common Prayer: A Liturgy for Ordinary Radicals* (Grand Rapids, MI: Zondervan, 2010). This book of daily prayers provides an excellent resource for people of all ages, but particularly for young people. It has a strong emphasis on issues of justice and peace.

http://universalis.com. Universalis contains the traditional texts of the Liturgy of the Hours from the Catholic tradition. The material from the website can also be found on the Laudate app, which can be downloaded for free.

Lectio Divina (chapter 3)

Enzo Bianchi, *Lectio Divina: From God's Word to Our Lives* (Brewster, MA: Paraclete Press, 2015). This is an excellent introduction to the history and practice of Lectio Divina.

https://www.pray-as-you-go.org/home/. Pray as You Go offers daily Lectio-style meditations from the community of Irish Jesuit priests. It is also available as a downloadable app for your phone.

Contemplative Prayer (chapter 4)

Thomas Merton, *Contemplative Prayer* (New York: Doubleday, 1996). Originally written in 1969, this is Merton's
premier text on contemplation and the life of a monk.
The 1996 edition includes an introduction from Merton's
friend Thich Nhat Hanh.

https://cac.org/. The Center for Contemplation and Action
(CAC) was founded by Richard Rohr, who seeks ways
to help people live contemplative lives in the midst of a
busy world.

Service (chapter 5)

https://habitat.org. The website for Habitat for Humanity contains a wealth of information about how to get
involved with this organization. Collegiate ministries will
be particularly interested in their "Collegiate Challenge,"
which coordinates college alternative spring break trips.

http://www.umcmission.org/Get-Involved/Volunteer
-Opportunities/About-UMVIM. United Methodist Volunteers in Mission do service projects all around the
world through Global Ministries.

http://www.umcor.org/. The United Methodist Committee
on Relief (UMCOR) provides practical assistance during
and after natural disasters.

Spiritual Direction (chapter 6)

John O'Donohue, *Anam Cara: A Book of Celtic Wisdom* (New
York: HarperCollins, 1998). Although not a traditional
text on spiritual direction, this is a lyrical introduction to
the Celtic concept of anam cara, or "soul friend."

http://www.sdiworld.org/. The online home of Spiritual Directors International.

Pilgrimage (chapter 7)

Paulo Coelho, *The Pilgrimage* (San Francisco: HarperCollins, 1992). Coelho's autobiographical novel about a pilgrim on the Camino de Santiago inspires many to rediscover this ancient route.

The Way, Icon Entertainment International, directed by Emilio Estevez, 2010. Starring Estevez and his father, Martin Sheen, this film follows a heartbroken father (Sheen) who seeks to complete a journey on the Camino that was begun by his son (Estevez). A moving portrayal of life on the Camino and the community that can be found on the trail.

http://www.wm.edu/sites/pilgrimage/. The Institute for Pilgrimage Studies at William and Mary holds a yearly conference and symposium on pilgrimage and publishes numerous articles on the topic. In addition, William and Mary sponsors study-abroad opportunities for students who wish to study pilgrimage in places such as Santiago de Campostela.

Intentional Community (chapter 8)

Rimes McElveen, "Wesley, Integrity, and Vocation: The Power and Possibility of Collegiate Intentional Christian Communities," in *The Prophetic Voice and Making Peace,* ed. Matthew Charlton and Kathryn Armistead (Nashville: General Board of Higher Education and Ministry, 2016). This article is an excellent introduction to the concept of intentional community on college campuses and explores the work of Vista House at Furman.

David Janzen, *The Intentional Christian Community Handbook: For Idealists, Hypocrites, and Wannabe Disciples of Jesus* (Brewster, MA: Paraclete Press, 2013). David Janzen, one of the leaders of the Reba Place Fellowship in Chicago, Illinois, lays out some of the practical and theological considerations for those who wish to engage in intentional community.

Hospitality (chapter 9)

Timothy Fry, OSB, ed., *The Rule of St. Benedict in English* (Collegeville, MN: Liturgical Press, 1982). Saint Benedict's *Rule* is the definitive authority for Benedictine communities, which would make it a good candidate for a resource on intentional community. The *Rule* also has extensive writings on the topic of hospitality, which is a big part of the Benedictine charism.

Christine D. Pohl, *Making Room: Recovering Hospitality as a Christian Tradition* (Grand Rapids, MI: Eerdmans, 1999). Pohl, who is a professor of church and society and Christian ethics at Asbury, introduces the reader to the role that hospitality played in the ancient church and explores how that tradition continues in the contemporary church. A good read for background on the meaning of hospitality within the Christian tradition.

CPSIA information can be obtained
at www.ICGtesting.com
Printed in the USA
FFHW021522021218
49697549-54098FF